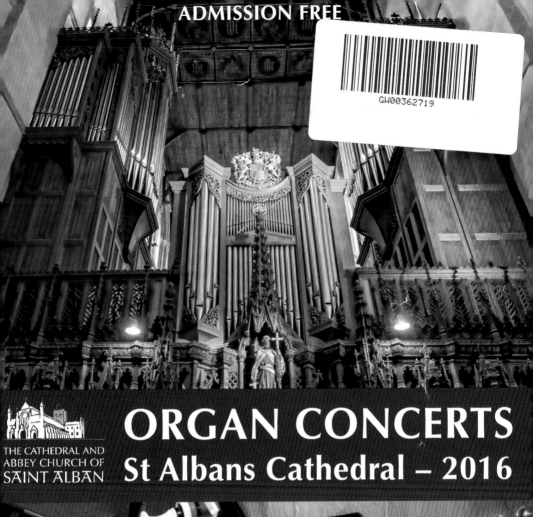

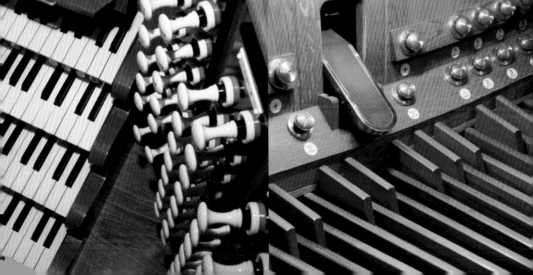

ORGAN CONCERTS
St Albans Cathedral – 2016

THE CATHEDRAL AND
ABBEY CHURCH OF
SAINT ALBAN

Wednesday Lunchtime Organ Concerts 2016
12.30–1.05 pm in St Albans Cathedral

Admission free

13 January
Linden Innes-Hopkins
(Organist and Director of Music, St John's, Boxmoor)

3 February
Tom Bell
(Organist, St Michael's, Chester Square, London)

9 March
Rachel Mahon
(Organ Scholar, St Paul's Cathedral, London)

20 April
Jonathan Vaughn
(Assistant Organist, Wells Cathedral)

18 May
Tom Etheridge
(Senior Organ Scholar, King's College, Cambridge)

15 June
Nicholas Freestone
(Organ Scholar, St Albans Cathedral)

28 September
Tim Harper
(Assistant Director of Music, Ripon Cathedral)

12 October
Alexander Flood
(Assistant Director of Music, St Peter's Church, St Albans)

9 November
Roger Judd
(Sub Organist, St Laurence, Ludlow)

Admission to the concerts is free.
A retiring collection helps to support music in the Cathedral.

For information on St Albans Cathedral and forthcoming events,
go to: www.stalbanscathedral.org

THE ORGANS AND MUSICIANS OF ST ALBANS CATHEDRAL

Andrew Lucas

PUBLISHED BY THE FRATERNITY OF THE FRIENDS OF ST ALBANS ABBEY

ACKNOWLEDGEMENTS

I am greatly indebted to Dr Peter Hurford for his kindness in allowing me to draw extensively upon his history *The Organs of St Albans Abbey* (1963 and later editions). It is impossible to better the characterful turns of phrase which pepper his writing (for an example see the opening paragraph). Consequently I have, for the most part, retained his wording in the first six chapters, adding new material where necessary.

Hurford in turn drew upon *A History of the Organs at the Cathedral of St Alban* (up to 1929) by G. C. Straker and much information from Straker's work has been re-instated in this book.

Sincere thanks also go to others who have willingly given invaluable help and advice in the preparation of this book, in particular Mrs. Pat Hurford, who provided further helpful information regarding the consultation process for the 1962 organ and clarified dates; Mark Venning, Managing Director of Harrison & Harrison for additional technical information; Kathryn Beecroft, Michael Bowden, Ailsa Herbert, Tom Winpenny and Alexander Woodrow for their assistance with the reading of the proofs; Dr David Kelsall, Hon. Archivist for providing photographs and other images from the Cathedral Archives; and Malcolm Bury, Alan Herbert, Mark Jameson and Dr Simon Lindley for providing additional photographs.

Andrew Lucas, April 2009

SOURCES

Bicknell, Stephen: *The History of the English Organ* (Cambridge, 1996)

Clutton, Cecil, and Niland, Austin: *The British Organ* (London, 1963 and later editions)

Downes, Ralph: *Baroque Tricks* (Oxford, 1983)

Elvin, Laurence: *The Harrison Story* (Lincoln, 1974)

Hurford, Peter: *The Organs of St. Albans Abbey* (St Albans, 1963 and later editions)

McLachlan, D.: *Dr L.G. Hayne and the Organs of Bradfield and Mistley* (1992) (http://www.archerfamily.org.uk/bio/hayne_lg.html)

Straker, G.C.: *A History of the Organs at the Cathedral of St. Alban* (London, c. 1940)

Straker, G.C. and Willis, Henry III: *The Organs of St. Albans Abbey: The Rotunda, Volume 3, No. 1* (London, September 1929)

Sumner, Prof. W. L.: *The Organ: Its Construction, Evolution and Principles of Use* (London, 1952)

Watkins Shaw, Dr. H.: *The Succession of Organists* (Oxford, 1991)

Thistlethwaite, Rev'd Canon Dr Nicholas: *The Making of the Victorian Organ* (Cambridge, 1990)

West, John E.: *Cathedral Organists Past and Present* (London, 1899 and later editions)

The Leffler Notebooks (1800) (British Organ Archive)

CONTENTS

*A view of the organ loft in 2009
from the clerestory, showing the
console in its new position, the north
case and the rear of the Choir Organ
case with its shutters open.
(photograph by David Kelsall)*

CHAPTER 1

THE EARLY ORGANS OF
ST ALBANS ABBEY (1300–1820)

In the beginning the organist was Adam, who is named as one of the contributors to a feast given on the election of John de Maryns as Abbot in 1302. If Adam had a predecessor we do not know his name, and it seems an appropriate name for the first of the line.

We know that in 1380 there was an organ in the Chapel of St Mary, made by John of Yarmouth, one of the monks, and an organ is again mentioned in an account of the installation of John de la Moote as Abbot in 1396: ' *... the sermon ended, the hymn Te Deum Laudamus was solemnly and devoutly chanted by the Convent, the organs alternating.'* [1]

There may have been a general decline in the music in the Abbey by the early fifteenth century because we learn that in 1421 a monk deserted St Albans to join the monastery at Christchurch, Canterbury, simply to enjoy opportunities of studying the art. However John of Wheathampstead, who was elected Abbot in 1420, went to great pains to improve the services and in 1423 appointed two paid organists. [2]

In medieval times the abbot conferred membership of the Fraternity of St Albans Abbey on pilgrims whose generosity to the Abbey merited this high privilege. Members would usually be admitted to the Fraternity in person and this is likely to have been quite an occasion. A contemporary Book of Benefactors of the Abbey tells us about one of those accepted into the Fraternity:

'In 1422, on the morrow of St Laurence, John Kyllyngworthe of Gloucester, the quality organ maker of his day, received in person the benefit of the fraternity of our chapter…He let us off 5 marks for organs bought from him.'

In 1428 Wheathampstead also had an organ (costing £17 6s. 8d.[3]) set up in the choir on a wooden structure (pulpitum) which had been erected some time before for the reading of the Gospel; and again in 1438, he presented to the church a *'payre of organes'*[4] costing over £50 and said to be the largest in England. This organ was set up in the position previously occupied by the pulpitum. When this larger organ was erected, the smaller organ was removed to the Retro-Choir (now the Lady Chapel), where Mass with musical accompaniment was celebrated daily. Wheathampstead's Registrum gives a eulogistic account of the new large organ in language dizzily compounded from Psalms 149 and 150:

'That young men and maidens, and old people besides, as well as the younger, should be able to praise the Lord of Heaven and extol Him in the highest, not indeed with the drum and dance, but with stringed instruments and the organ and its pipes, and a sound as of sweet voiced cymbals, he [the Abbot] caused to be made a pair of organs, than which there were not readily to be found, as was believed, an instrument more beautiful to look upon, or more sweet to hear, or more elaborate in workmanship in any monastery throughout the whole kingdom. As to its cost, in the making and fixing it in position, more than fifty pounds was spent.'[5]

It is most likely that it was upon this same praiseworthy organ that England's illustrious musician, Robert Fayrfax, would have played at the beginning of the sixteenth century.

---

[1] The custom of alternating verses of a hymn with passages of organ music was common at this time.

[2] Nor was he probably above a little bribery in his enthusiasm, for the Bishop of Durham is said to have had suspicions that a singing boy had been enticed away from his Chapel to St Albans

[3] Worth approximately £90,000 in modern currency

[4] Singular, as in 'a pair of bellows'. This organ would cost about £250,000 today, implying a substantially larger instrument than the previous organ.

[5] Translation by the late Dean Lawrance for an article in the Musical Times, 1909.

In the accounts of the monastery for 1529–30, amongst items for mowing nettles, catching moles and supplying cords for the bells, is an amount of 7s. 6d. paid to John Dapton for mending the organs. The fees and wages paid in that same year to the Chief Steward, Solicitor, Abbot's Secretary and the organist amounted to £74 13s. 6d.[6] The organist mentioned here was Henry Besteney, who at the dissolution of the monastery received a pension of two marks a year and his board.

Before 1 November 1552, all the organs seem to have disappeared, as in an inventory made on that date, no mention is made of any organ (though St Peter's Church is stated as still possessing a 'payre of organes'), and there is no record of any other organ at the Abbey until 1820. In any case in the unhappy period of the Civil War (1642–51), Parliamentary Ordinances of 1643–1644 order that, amongst other things, 'organ frames and cases should be taken away and defaced'.

After the dissolution of the monastery (on 5 December 1539) the Abbey Church was sold in 1553 to the townspeople of St Albans for £400, who adapted part of it for parochial use. After that, musical services for three centuries seem to have been of a very restricted nature, the only accompaniment to the singing being that of sundry musical instruments other than an organ, when players were available.

In 1706 the name of Jeremiah Hopkins is recorded as 'Musician'. A long obituary notice of John Kent in the *Gentleman's Magazine* of 1798 sheds interesting light upon the service music during the eighteenth century. A plumber and glazier by trade, Kent held the office of Parish Clerk of the Abbey for nearly 52 years until his death in 1798 aged 80.

A painting of John Kent (from a print in the Cathedral Archives)

'In his official station as parish clerk it may not be presumption to say that in psalmody he was excelled by no one, and equalled by few, particularly in the Old Hundredth Psalm. He had a voice strong and melodious, and was himself a complete master of church musick; always pleased to hear the congregation join. It has been often remarked, when country choristers came from a neighbouring parish to perform in the Abbey, with instruments, termed by him a box of whistles, with which the congregation could not join, he, on those occasions, gave out the Psalm or Anthem in this way: "Sing YE to the praise and glory of God." ... His last essay was on a public occasion, Monday, Sept. 10, that of the consecration of a pair of colours presented to that spirited corps the St. Alban's Volunteers, by the Hon. Miss Grimstons, when he sang the Twentieth Psalm before one of the most respectable congregations that ever assembled within those sacred walls.'[7]

The Churchwardens' accounts of a later period show that the accompaniments to the services at that time were supplied by orchestral instruments which were played by 'Pantamus,' Thomas John and Sander Higdon, and John Eagleton. We find the following entry on 25 December 1814:

Paid John Higdon, ½ yrs. salary for playing the clarionet at the church on Sundays £4 4s. 0d.

Many similar entries, some at an interval of three months, show that Mr Higdon received eight guineas a year for his services.

6 These four salaries have an equivalent current value of £350,000, indicating the importance of these posts.

7 *Gentleman's Magazine*, Oct. 1798, 905-7.

CHAPTER 2
THE EARLY NINETEENTH CENTURY (1820–1860)

At a court held on 2 April 1819, the St Albans Corporation 'concurred on the application of the Reverend Mr Small, Rector,' in an effort to provide an organ for the Abbey Church by subscription.

1820-1833
The Smith and Byfield organ in its original position on the gallery to the east of the rood screen (from a print in the Cathedral Archives)

On 23 April the Corporation subscribed £20 towards a second-hand organ from the church of St Dunstan-in-the-East, London by Bernard 'Father' Smith and John Byfield, the total cost of which was £450.

Originally built by 'Father' Smith in 1670 as a one manual organ (the Great Organ). 'Mr. Bernard Smith, organist, who dwelleth in Suffolk Street over against the Cock' received £10 a year for repairing and cleaning his own work. The Choir and Swell organs were added at a later date by John Byfield who also carried out various alterations. This instrument was described in Dr E. J. Hopkins' manuscript Organ Book as 'a very fine instrument, particularly the Open Diapason on the great organ.' Leffler[8] in

1800 describes it as possessing 'Three setts of keys; compass GG to D, short octaves, swell down to Fiddle G.'[9] and that 'The Swell one of the best in London'.

Specification of the organ in St Dunstan-in the East, London

Great Organ
52 notes from GG (short octave) to d in alt.
Open Diapason
Stopped Diapason
Principal
Fifteenth
Sesquialtera 3 ranks
Trumpet
Clarion
Cornet 3 ranks (from middle c).

Swell Organ
32 notes from fiddle G to d in alt.
Open Diapason
Principal
Cornet 3 ranks
Trumpet
Hautboy

Choir Organ
52 notes – compass as the Great Organ
Stopped Diapason
Principal
Cremona
Vox Humana

---

[8] Straker listed this from the notebook of J. H. Leffler, organist of St Katherine-by-the-Tower, London, made in 1800. It was Leffler's hobby to travel around the country examining various organs and noting down their specifications and conditions, therefore we have the details of the 'Father' Smith organ as it stood in 1800.

[9] The compass of organ keyboards has changed over the centuries. GG is the bass note five semitones below the present standard bottom note C, whose speaking length for an organ pipe is 8 feet. Fiddle G is one octave and a half higher than 8' C and is the same as the bottom note of the violin, hence the term fiddle G; d in alt (altissimo) is the top note 7 notes lower than the top note on the modern cathedral organ.

The organem was erected in the Abbey by Mr George Gray, who later built a new organ for St Dunstan's church. It stood on a wooden gallery immediately to the east of the fourteenth century stone rood screen[10], and is described as having a fine old oak Gothic case with double front (i.e. west and east fronts) and four spires, and a black keyboard with white sharps. It was first used on 25 June 1820, although it was not publicly opened until 26 November.

Specification of the organ as installed by Gray in 1820 in St Albans Abbey

Gray added to the Smith/Byfield organ the following stops: Great – Twelfth; Swell – Stopped Diapason (in place of the Cornet); Choir – Nason Flute and Fifteenth (in place of the Vox Humana). In addition, the 1820 organ contained a Pedal stop.

Great Organ 52 notes (GG–d, short octaves)

Open Diapason (metal)	8
Open Diapason (wood)	8
Principal (metal)	4
Twelfth (metal)	2⅔
Fifteenth (metal)	2
Sesquialtra* (3 ranks, 17, 19, 22) (metal)	
Cornet* (3 ranks, 12, 15 17) (metal)	
Trumpet (metal)	8
Clarion (metal)	4
(*divided at middle C)	

Swell Organ 32 notes (fiddle G–d)

Open Diapason	8
Stopped Diapason	8
Principal	4
Trumpet	8
Hautboy	8

Choir Organ 52 notes (GG–d, short octaves)

Stopped Diapason (wood)	8
Nason Flute (wood)	(4?)[12]
Principal (metal)	4
Fifteenth (metal)	2
Cremona (metal)	8

Pedal Organ (GG–? Compass unknown)

Open Diapason (wood)[11]

There was compiled specially for use at the services a little book of 156 pages, entitled: *A Selection of Psalms, and Hymns adapted for the use of the Abbey Church, St. Albans, 1820* containing a selection of metrical psalms, 76 hymns and four doxologies. It was compiled by Mr Thomas Fowler, the organist who, as such, received the sum of £31 10s. 0d. a year, while the blower received £10 a year.

1835-1860
A print showing the organ in the north transept as rebuilt by Bevington (from a print in the Cathedral Archives)

---

10 That is, where the current organ gallery is sited. The gallery was originally two bays further east (and immediately west of the tower). It was moved in 1820 to carry the newly acquired organ.

11 It is presumed that this would have sounded at 8′ pitch – the longest pipe therefore having a theoretical speaking length of about 11 feet)

12 It is not clear from the records available but it would be reasonable to assume that this was at 4′ pitch, which is the most common form of this stop, rather than 8′ as reported in earlier histories of the organ

In the early 1830s urgent repairs to the fabric were needed and the Sunday services took place in the Lady Chapel. In 1833 this organ was removed from its gallery and it lay for two years on the floor of the Presbytery. It was rebuilt in 1835 by Henry Bevington and placed in the north transept on its original nave gallery, the west (back) front of the case being disposed of at this time. On 23 August 1835 the Abbey Church was re-opened by the Bishop of London after some restoration. A collection for the rebuilding of the organ amounted to £104 but the organ was not completed until the end of the year. It seems to have been opened on 31 December when the collections amounted to £10 2s. 2d. after deducting £5 for expenses. The amount collected by voluntary subscriptions was £161 5s. 6d. There are some curious entries in the Churchwardens' accounts for this period:

1835-1860
Another view of the organ in the north transept, possibly more accurately represented than in the previous print (Cathedral Archives)

Oct. 29th, 1821.
Paid John Warwick for new surplices
for the Charity Children
£6 14s. 9d.
Thos. Fowler (organist) for music books
£2 12s. 6d.

June 17th, 1824.
Paid Mr. John Gray for Tuneing the organ
£12 5s. 0d.

Mar. 25th, 1825.
Paid Mr. John Gray for Tuneing the organ
£5 17s. 2d.

May 28th, 1828.
Given to the Singers to pay attention to the Organist
1s. 0d.

July 19th, 1828.
Paid Mr. Nicholls half year's salary for Tuneing the organ
£4 0s. 0d.
and for opening and repairing the diapason pipes
£3 3s. 0d.

Aug. 15th, 1833.
Fowler on account of his services at the chapel
£9 0s. 0d.
(i.e. the Lady Chapel where services were taking place during the restoration of the church fabric).

This organ supported the services in the part of the Abbey which was being used for services (east of the ancient nave screen) until 1860. During this period the nave remained unused and gradually fell into dangerous disrepair.

CHAPTER 3

THE HILL ORGAN (1861)

In 1861 a new three manual organ was built by William Hill from a specification drawn up by the organist, John Booth, and approved by Dr E. J. Hopkins, organist of the Temple Church in London. The organ cost over £1,100 exclusive of the value of the Open Diapason to tenor C from the old Father Smith organ. The old organ was sold to St Lawrence Church, Bradfield, Essex, and at one time was thought to have formed part of a rather eccentric three-manual instrument designed by the late Dr L. G. Hayne, a former Rector, in the 1870s.[13]

The new organ was installed on the floor of the north transept and because it was significantly larger than the previous instrument[14] the gallery, on which had stood the old organ, was scrapped. Also, whereas the old organ had retained the old-fashioned long compass, inherited from Smith, Hill's new instrument had the modern (German) compass for both the manuals and pedals, that is the manuals had 56 notes from CC to G on all three manuals, whilst the compass of the Pedal Organ was 30 notes from CCC to F. A significant number of pipes from the Hill instrument survive in the cathedral organ to the present day, although their voicing has been altered by subsequent organ builders.

Sounding from a place in front of the back wall of the north transept, one of the most resonant spaces in the building, this must have been a grand instrument which sounded well in the areas then used for Divine Worship (the quire, transepts and presbytery, which lead from the space under the great tower). With its much greater variety of colour and intensity of sound it would have been a dramatic development from the old organ for both the organist and the listener, and there is little doubt that it charmed most who heard it. Locally, the Swell Organ was considered to be practically unrivalled, 'being rather superior to the immense new organ in St Paul's Cathedral'.[15]

1861-1871
The Hill organ on the floor of the north transept
(photograph by F. Downer of Watford, by kind permission of Mark Jameson)

---

13 It is now considered more likely that Hayne's organ was new and that the organ from St Albans went to another church in London's east end
  - see D. McLachlan: *Dr L G Hayne and the Organs of Bradfield and Mistley* (1992)

14 Length: 22ft; Width: 19ft; Height to the top of swell box: 23ft 3in. The number of speaking stops increased from 20 (Gray) to 38 (Hill).

15 Straker, page 7. The actual source of this remark is not given.

The façade, consisting of unframed and seemingly unsupported bass pipes, had no real case structure. It was designed by the Rector, the Revd Dr H. D. Nicholson, whose aim was for it to be in keeping with the architectural style of the north transept. In reality it was rather plain and ugly and certainly does not compare well with the elegant profile of its predecessor.[16]

On 27 July 1861 several hundred people assembled in the Abbey and were delighted to hear 'a quarter of an hour's practice' by the Abbey organist, Mr Booth. The formal celebration of the installation of the organ came on 1 August with two services, at 11am and 3pm, and an organ recital after the second service. The performers were the organist Mr Booth, with Mr Pitts (organist of Brompton Oratory) and Mr Schroder (from St Peter's Church in St Albans). The programme of the music performed reveals the taste of the times.

The last Anthem was O Praise God, with solos for Miss Cox and Mr Henry (from Her Majesty's Chapel Royal), and it was commented at the time that the accompaniments were 'charmingly played on the Harmonic Flute, Trumpet and Clarion Stops!'[17] The grandeur of the

MORNING SERVICE at 11.
(Mr. Booth at the Organ.)

Introd. Voluntary – "Kyrie" (3rd Mass)	Haydn
Venite	Grand Chant
Gloria – Chant	Bennet in F
Te Deum – Chant	Lawes in C
Jubilate – Chant	Attwood in A
Anthem – "O Praise God in His Holiness"	Dr. Clarke Whitfeld
Psalm before Sermon	"Old Hundredth"
Concluding Voluntary – "Coronation Anthem"	Handel

AFTERNOON at 3.

Introd. Voluntary – "Cujus animam"	
Litany	Tallis

COLLECTION

Organ Concerto (Rinck) and March (Mendelssohn)	Mr. Booth
Anthem – "O give thanks "	Purcell
Organ Symphony (Beethoven)	Mr. Pitts
Anthem – "Sleepers, wake"	Mendelssohn
Organ – "They have not known Thee"	(Schroder)
Occasional Overture (Handel)	Mr. Schroder
Anthem – "The Lord of Might"	Hon. Miss Grosvenor
Organ – "Air, varied" (Adolphus Hess)	Mr. Pitts
Anthem – "Hear my Prayer"	Kent
Organ – "Unto Thee, O Lord" (Schroder) and March (Schumann)	Mr. Schroder
Anthem – "Hallelujah"	Handel
Organ – "God Save the Queen" (Rinck)	Mr. Booth

---

[16] The front pipes made by Hill for this case were reused as the front pipes for the north case at the division of the organ in the early twentieth century and remained in the north façade until the organ was dismantled in 2007.

[17] Straker, page 8. Again the actual source of this remark is not given, though it may well be from accounts in the local press at the time.

sound of this organ was greatly appreciated by those present. The Abbey Choir was joined on this occasion by other singers to make a choir of about 80 voices – this was a grand occasion indeed.

The collection amounted to the tremendous sum of £105 14s. 2¼d. Subscriptions flowed in and it was recorded that on 3 August the required sum of £1,100[18] was reached, owing in no small part to the hard work and charismatic leadership of the Rector, Dr Nicholson.

Specification of the new organ by William Hill installed in the north transept in 1861

This stoplist is from Straker's *History*. Variants are listed in a footnote[19]

Great Organ	ft	pipes	Choir Organ	ft	pipes
Double Open Diapason	16	56	Lieblich Gedact	8	56
Open Diapason	8	56	Cone Gamba	8	56
Open Diapason (Father Smith)	8	56	Dulciana (to tenor C)	8	44
Gamba	8	56	Gemshorn	4	56
Stopped Diapason	8	56	Wald Flute	4	56
Principal	4	56	Flautina	2	56
Harmonic Flute	4	56	Cremona	8	56
Twelfth	3	56			
Fifteenth	2	56	**Pedal Organ**		
Full Mixture, 3 ranks		168	Open Diapason (wood)	16	30
Sharp Mixture, 3 ranks		168	Violone (wood)	16	30
Posaune	8	56	Bourdon (wood)	16	30
Clarion	4	56	Principal	8	30
			Trombone (wood)	16	30
Swell Organ					
Bourdon	16	56	**Pipe summary:**		
Open Diapason	8	56	Great:	952	
Keraulophon (to tenor C)	8	44	Swell:	828	
Rohr Gedact	8	56	Choir:	380	
Principal	4	56	Pedal:	150	
Rohr Flute	4	56	Total:	2,310	
Twelfth	3	56			
Fifteenth	2	56	There were 38 speaking stops, five couplers and		
Mixture, 3 ranks		168	a set of five composition pedals (no details are		
Double Trumpet	16	56	given) to assist with registration.		
Horn	8	56			
Hautboy	8	56	The compass was C–g3 for the manuals and C–f1		
Clarion	4	56	for the pedal keyboard.		
Tremulant					

---

[18] Currently worth £686,000, and roughly the same cost as a comparable new instrument today. The sum raised in the collections was about 10% of that value, and gives us an idea of the financial success of the opening concerts.

[19] Variants: In Thistlethwaite, *The Making of the Victorian Organ* (Cambridge University Press, 1990) there are a few differences in nomenclature: the Choir and Swell have Stopped Diapasons instead of the Gedacts, the Swell gives a Double Diapason 16′ for the Bourdon, the Choir a Clarionet rather than Cremona, and Swell Oboe for Hautboy. Thistlethwaite also gives the more correct German word Flöte for the Wald Flute and Rohr Flute and notes that the Choir 2′ stop is called Flautino. An undated manuscript in the cathedral archive mentions that the Choir Gemshorn was initially prepared for and that the Choir 2′ consisted of stopped pipes, though this seems unlikely.

The Choir and Musical Record (1863) tells us that

> 'There is a firmness, nervousness and resonant ring about the whole organ that is eminently satisfactory; and this character extends even to the Choir Organ, the part that in nearly all new English organs is so weak and insignificant, but which in this example, is as lively and spirited as the best specimens to be met with occasionally in old organs.'

No doubt inspired by this new acquisition, music making in the Abbey flourished in this period.

In July 1862 there was a Music Festival and on Easter Day 1863 Hymns Ancient and Modern was adopted. There were further Music Festivals in 1863 and 1865 and then in October 1866 the first Festival of St Albans Choral Union was held, the music being 'Gregorian'.

From 1867, it was decided that the psalms were now to be chanted at both Sunday services using Monk and Ouseley's Psalter and the choir now numbered some 30 voices. In July 1867 the second Festival of the Choral Union was held in the nave. An organ by Walker was erected in the north aisle and a platform erected for the 600 choristers who took part.[20] By 1871 anthems were regularly sung at the 3pm Sunday service, services at this time being at 11am, 3pm and 6.15pm.

1871-1881
The Hill organ in the north nave aisle (from the Cathedral Archives) - see chapter 4

[20] These festivals were intended to be after the model of the Three Choirs at Hereford, Gloucester and Worcester and hoped to become a permanent institution, but financial constraints arose owing to no charge being made for admission, whilst the proceeds were not sufficient to defray the expenses.

CHAPTER 4

THE ABBEY BECOMES A CATHEDRAL AND THE ORGAN IS RESTORED (1871–1908)

For more than 30 years no services had been held in the nave because of its bad state of repair; but in 1871 preparations were being made to restore the whole Abbey and in order that work could be done on the north transept, services were started again in the nave. Accordingly in June that year the organ was moved from the north transept by Hill & Son and rebuilt in the second arch west of the nave screen on the north side, as can be seen from the contemporary photograph on the previous page.

It had been feared that, in order to fit the instrument to this position, it would be necessary to leave out the Swell and part of the Pedal Organ owing to insufficient space being available. But the difficulty was overcome by Hill, who made the front of the organ project several feet from the pillars, and extended the external structure on each side, thus enabling the instrument to be rebuilt complete.[21]

By 1877, restoration of the transept was complete and work began on the nave; services were restored to the north transept and, rather than move the organ yet again, another organ was hired from Hill at a cost of £25 a year. This was sited in the transept and used to accompany services. Meanwhile, the organ in the nave was silent and was being suffocated with stone dust. After four years in this state, the organ was removed once again in 1881 to sit on a gallery 15 feet above the floor level adjacent to the stone nave altar screen, where the temporary organ had been. The ungainly Hill façade (with the console below it, *en fenêtre*[22]) faced to the east and the back of the organ, which was originally hidden against the rear wall of the north transept, revealed the working innards of the organ in all their glory to anyone in the nave.

1888-1908
The pipes added by Abbott & Smith to the west façade (from the Cathedral Archives)

To defray expenses, a total of £213 19s. 9d. was received by subscriptions and an offertory.[23] The organ was re-opened after a short service and address by the Rector, the Revd Walter Lawrance. The choir was augmented from Mr George Gaffe's Vocal Class and numbered 100 voices. They were accompanied by Dr A. H. Mann, organist of King's College, Cambridge, who also performed Mendelssohn's Sixth Organ Sonata.

---

21 The Churchwardens' accounts from Easter, 1866, to Easter, 1867, include the following items: Organist's salary, £31 4s. 0d. Paid Organ Blower, £3 0s. 0d. Paid second ditto, 10s. 0d. Fire Insurance for organ from Christmas, 1866, to Christmas, 1867, £2 5s. 0d. Paid Hill & Son from Midsummer, 1866, to Midsummer, 1867, £10 0s. 0d.

22 En fenêtre - literally in the window. Used as a technical term for 'attached' organ consoles as opposed to 'detached' as the present cathedral organ.

23 This was spent as follows: Mr. C. Miskin, for Gallery front and staircase, £93 2s. 0d., Chappell & Co., Hire of Harmonium, £4 19s. 0d., Hill & Son, removing and repairing organ, £110, Stevens, for printing, £4 4s. 4d., Carpenter, for organ fittings, £1 0s. 0d., Carriage of Harmonium, 8s. 10d., Messengers, 5s. 0d., Balance to offertory, 7d.

It was in 1877 also that the Abbey Church became the Cathedral of the new Diocese of St Albans and services were soon held in both quire and nave. Although the Hill organ sounded well in its new position for services in the quire, because all the Great Organ pipes and the Swell box projected their sound eastwards, the situation in the nave was far from satisfactory and the organ was found to be inadequate for its new responsibilities.

Consequently Lord Grimthorpe[24] (who had been architecturally and financially responsible for restoring the Abbey) arranged for it to be remodelled and enlarged in 1885, and a new west front of 16´ metal pipes[25] was added by Mr Abbott of Leeds, thus saving the congregation in the nave from an unsightly view of the Swell box and preserving the instrument's modesty. At the same time, the console was moved to the south side of the organ so that the organist could keep a watchful eye on the choristers, whether they were singing in choir or nave.

With the restoration of the Abbey so fresh, pride in the building was rekindled, and there were soon complaints that the organ in the centre of the screen was spoiling the view down the length of the Church. Two articles in the local newspaper tell the story of the next stage in the organ's history.

On Wednesday Lord Aldenham visited St Albans Cathedral … and when passing through the building with Canon Wigram, he glanced up at the Organ and remarked that its division so as to extend the vista to the unique Wallingford screen [behind the High Altar] was an improvement greatly to be desired … The division of the Organ into two parts and its connection with a keyboard on the floor of the Cathedral so as to bring the Organist into closer touch with the Choir would be a matter of very great expense, and with the calls that are being made at the present time in connection with the development of the Diocesan organisation, there are no funds available.
(Herts Advertiser, 1 September 1906)

We understand that Lord Aldenham has most generously expressed his desire to bear the whole of the cost of the alterations of the Organ of St Albans Cathedral by dividing it so that the whole space above St Cuthbert's Screen [the stone screen] in the Nave, occupied by the present instrument, will be left vacant and a direct view will be obtained from west to east. The intention in building the Organ is to place it against the north & south walls of the Choir at the same level as at present, extending probably not more than four feet out on each side, and it is hoped that several new stops may be added. The larger pipes will be laid down flat on the floor of the present organ chamber, and the organist's seat will be in somewhat the same position as at present. Designs for these alterations have been prepared by Messrs Abbott & Smith, organ builders of Leeds and it is probable that the work will soon be begun. Mr J Oldrid Scott will, in all probability, be asked to design a simple casing for the pipes when they are placed in position.
(Herts Advertiser, 29 December 1906)

Lord Aldenham[26] was indeed generous, as this dividing of the organ into two cases at the side of the organ loft involved a major rebuild, costing £3,000. The work was started in 1907 by Messrs Abbott and Smith of Leeds to a specification prepared by Sir Hugh Allen. The new oak cases (which still exist to the

---

24 Edmund Beckett Denison, 1st Baron Grimthorpe, (1816–1905) was a lawyer and an amateur horologist and architect. In 1851 he designed the mechanism for the clock and chimes of Big Ben at the Palace of Westminster in London. He was also responsible for the less than sympathetic rebuilding of St Albans Abbey, principally changing the west front, the transepts including replacing the large mediaeval windows in all three, and changing the profile of the roof of the entire building, all at his own expense. Although the building had been in need of urgent repair, popular opinion at the time held that he had changed the cathedral's character. Thus the contemporary verb 'to grimthorpe', meaning to carry out unsympathetic restorations of ancient buildings, enjoyed popularity for a while. He was not a humble man ('I am the only architect with whom I have never quarrelled.') and he included his own likeness in the statues of the four evangelists around the western door (the statue of St Matthew has Beckett's face). He was severely critical of G. G. Scott's restoration work of the Abbey as he was of J. O. Scott's later work. He is buried in the Abbey churchyard.

25 Presumably these new metal pipes replaced Hill's original wooden Violone stop on the Pedal.

26 Henry Hucks Gibbs, (1819–1907), raised to the peerage as Lord Aldenham of Aldenham in 1896, was a banker and businessman, eventually becoming Governor of the Bank of England. Gibbs was also involved in politics and sat briefly as an MP for the City of London in the 1890s, and held the office of High Sheriff of Hertfordshire in 1884. He paid for the restoration of the High Altar screen and for the insertion of new statues, against which Grimthorpe was bitterly opposed (the originals having been destroyed by iconoclasts at the Reformation). They were old adversaries, and coming as they did from the two extreme ends of the Anglican tradition – Aldenham being a High Churchman whilst Grimthorpe was most definitely not – we can be certain that Aldenham's intervention and financial support for the division of the organ was not without a certain amount of personal satisfaction that the statues on High Altar screen might been seen from the full length of the nave.

present day) were placed in front of the main and triforium arches on the north and south ends of the nave screen and were designed by the cathedral architect, John Oldrid Scott, to blend with the recently installed episcopal throne and choir stalls in the quire. The original proposal to place the console on the floor of the cathedral did not materialize and the organist remained with his instrument in the loft. The organ was opened on 27 February 1908, short recitals being given by Sir Hugh Allen and the recently appointed Cathedral organist, Mr W. L. Luttman.

The work of dividing the organ achieved its main objective, which was the removal of the bulk of the organ from the centre of the nave screen to the sides, allowing a clear view from the back of the nave to the High Altar screen. The two Scott cases are, alongside those at Lichfield Cathedral, St John's College Cambridge and Selby Abbey, some of his best known. His organ case designs are considered to be more elegant, successful and mature than those designed by his more famous father, George Gilbert Scott. The latter was renowned for his restoration of several cathedrals in the nineteenth century, and both father and son worked on the restoration of St Albans Abbey. J.O. Scott's success lay in the production of organ cases which follow more faithfully the principles of good organ case design as exemplified in earlier European models.[27]

The cases were well made and handsomely decorated, with excellent carving and detail in the pipe shades and other fretted work. Nevertheless savings were made by re-using the pipes of both Hill and Abbot and Smith's east and west façades. This created an overall effect which was adequate but not entirely satisfactory, largely owing to the unfortunately heavy effect caused by the lines of

c.1905
A hand-coloured print showing the Hill organ façade just after J.O. Scott's new choir stalls had been installed but before the organ was divided (a postcard from the Cathedral Archives)

the pipe feet and mouths running in parallel with the fretted pipe shades. The appearance of these older pipes dulled over the years and by the end of the twentieth century their tarnished appearance emphasized another weakness – the cases looked stolid, largely owing to their depth in relation to their height.[28] They had to be designed to stand out from the cathedral walls sufficiently to enclose the internal pipework and mechanisms. Although the overall visual appearance was a major improvement on what was there before, the rest of the rebuilding of the organ seems to have left a lot to be desired.

[27] Clutton and Niland: *The British Organ* (1963)

[28] 'it is an illustration that such an arrangement has no chance of success unless the cases are fairly shallow, as at Westminster Abbey' (*Ibid.*)

Specification of the organ as rebuilt by Abbot and Smith (1908)

Great Organ

Double Open Diapason	16
Large Open Diapason (new)	8
Open Diapason No. 1	8
Open Diapason No. 2 (Father Smith)	8
Stopped Diapason	8
Gamba	8
Dulciana (new)	8
Harmonic Flute	4
Octave	4
Fifteenth	2
Mixture (3 ranks)	
Posaune (new)	8
Clarion (new)	4

Swell Organ

Lieblich Bourdon	16
Open Diapason	8
Violin Diapason (new)	8
Rohr Gedact	8
Viol d'Orchestre (new)	8
Voix Celestes (from tenor C)	8
Octave	4
Fifteenth	2
Mixture (3 ranks)	
Double Trumpet	16
Horn (new)	8
Oboe	8
Clarion (new)	4
Tremulant	

Couplers

Great to Pedals
Swell to Pedals
Choir to Pedals
Solo to Pedals
Swell to Great
Swell to Choir
Choir to Great
Solo to Great
Swell Octave
Swell Sub-Octave
Swell unison off
Choir Octave
Choir Sub-Octave
Choir Unison Off

Choir Organ

Open Diapason (new)	8
Cone Gamba	8
Dulciana (new)	8
Lieblich Gedact*	8
Gemshorn	4
Wald Flute*	4
Flautina*	2
Corno di Bassetto* (new)	16
Cremona*	8

*Enclosed in swell box.

Solo Organ

Doppel Flute* (new)	8
Concert Flute* (new)	4
French Horn* (new)	8
Orchestral Oboe* (new)	8
Cor Anglais* (new – free reed)	8
Tuba (new)	8

*Enclosed in swell box.

Pedal Organ

Sub Bass (new)	32
Harmonic Bass (new)	32
Open Diapason	16
Violone (metal, added in 1885)	16
Bourdon	16
Octave (metal)	8
Bass Flute (new)	8
Trombone	16

Accessories

Four composition pedals to Pedal
Three composition pedals to Swell
Four composition pistons to Great
Three composition pistons to Swell
Three composition pistons to Choir
Three composition pistons to Solo
(One Piston on each manual was adjustable.)
One reversible Great to Pedal composition pedal
(on and off)
Three Swell Pedals
New detached console on the screen.
Tubular pneumatic key and stop action.

Between 1908 and 1929
Horizontal pedal pipes on the floor of the organ loft
(from Straker's 'History')

The Choir and Solo Organs were placed higher up in the two new cases behind the display pipes, but the Great and Swell pipework was relocated at the bottom of the two new cases at the level of the loft floor, presumably because old soundboards and other structures were used in the new layout. The solid linenfold panels at the bottom of each case effectively sealed the fate of these sections of the organ – the tone from the pipes had to waft up through the organ structure and sound indirectly and the general effect was muffled, especially to a listener in the nave. After the splendid open position of the organ in the centre of the nave screen before the re-build it must have been very disappointing to hear the organ's effect being so diminished. To make matters worse the fine proportions and colour of Hill's choruses on the Great and Swell were sacrificed in preference to the fashion of the times by the addition of several more 8´stops in varying powers in place of some of the brighter sounding mutations and mixtures. In spite of the enlarging of the organ to four manual divisions and the addition of new pipework, the organ must have seemed but a shadow of its former self.

The original power for blowing was a 5 h.p. Crossley Gas Engine installed in the grounds, but this was rapidly superseded by electricity, an 8 h.p. motor being installed, though this soon appeared to be inadequate for its task. From early on the tubular pneumatic key mechanism gave trouble and was generally unsatisfactory. After a relatively short space of time certain defects had became more apparent and it became more and more sluggish.

In August 1921, after only some 13 years' use, work was done on the organ again and alterations to pipework were carried out by Messrs Tunks and Son: a new Open Diapason was placed on the Great Organ in place of the Dulciana; on the Choir a very narrow scaled Viole d'Orchestre replaced the Cone Gamba, and on the Swell, a Hohl Flute replaced the Violin Diapason. All Great and Swell reeds, together with the Tuba, had harmonic trebles added; and a new pedal board was installed to measurements recommended by the Royal College of Organists. It is possible that at this time the lower case panels were removed from the organ cases in order to let more sound out from the buried Great and Swell divisions.

But by 1928, after repeated patching of the mechanisms, it was obvious that further and more drastic action was necessary and tenders were sought for the complete rebuilding of the organ.

1908-1929
The Abbott & Smith console (from the Cathedral Archives)

CHAPTER 5
THE WILLIS REBUILD (1929)

Five organ builders quoted for the work done in 1929 and Mr Luttman, the organist, summarized their proposals.

Rushworth and Dreaper was the most expensive (£4,350) and for this they would install a new tubular pneumatic mechanism. They also proposed to move the Swell Organ (one presumes higher up in the case) and to install a new console. They declared the blowing apparatus inadequate and recommended a new blower and motor to provide heavy wind (Mr Luttman did not think that this seemed a satisfactory method but noted, with much greater pleasure, that their proposal contained some all-important new stops).

Harrison & Harrison quoted £3,565 plus £260 for new blowing apparatus. They also proposed to provide a new tubular pneumatic mechanism, new console, reconstruct the soundboards and swell boxes and revoice the whole organ, yet there was no mention of moving the Swell nor, more crucially for Mr Luttman, any new stops. Tunks quoted £580 for repairs to the action and other mechanisms only, and was clearly dismissed as a serious contender for the contract, whereas Frederick Rothwell asked for £3960 to raise both the Great and Swell Organs, fit electro-pneumatic action and provide a new console, presumably one in his own unique style.

Henry Willis & Sons quoted £3,000 and were awarded the contract. Their survey of 17 March 1928 states:

'the tubular pneumatic mechanism is truly deplorable, the design being very inferior. Precision of touch is lacking, the repetition is poor and the notes of the coupler mechanism frequently fail. It is impossible for the player to obtain proper results from mechanism of this nature. While careful regulation may improve matters to some small degree, the only real solution is to sweep away the tubular system and replace it by electro-pneumatic mechanism to ensure instant reliability.'

Regarding the tone of the organ:

'On the whole the material is good, but the treatment of the pipes and reeds not of a nature [for] obtaining the best results. In fact the tone of the organ is poor while the reeds are really bad. Many of the pipes are in a very bad state and require extensive repairs. Their condition is due to improper tuning methods used. By complete re-voicing and remodelling of certain stops a superb and glorious result would be obtained.'

Their solution was to provide electro-pneumatic action (guaranteed for 25 years) controlled from a new 'Willis' console. They offered to do the work in instalments if found desirable, but this would be more expensive in the long term. They proposed extending the manual compass to top C (61 notes), but it is less clear if the Swell Organ would be moved or remain at the same level. Mr Luttman's notes are unclear on this matter but he seemed more sure of other details:

'Tuba outside box, French Horn retained but made even throughout.'[29]

1929
The console of the Willis organ (from the Cathedral Archives)

29 In the end the Swell remained where it was, the Tuba was enclosed and the French Horn was scrapped.

Luttman was concerned about the new electro-pneumatic action and posed several questions about it including its predicted longevity (and well he might, as it turned out). There would be new rotary blowing machines (the normal fan 'blower' of today) adequate for raising the required amount of wind needed for the revoiced organ.

The Willis report was accepted and almost immediately, in August 1928, the new blowing apparatus with 7½ h.p. motor was installed. The remainder of the work commenced in January 1929. In an article written in 1929 for the firm's journal, The Rotunda, Henry Willis III explains that "*the replanning and revoicing of this organ proved quite the most difficult proposition that I have had to handle, and that the successful result has been a source of considerable satisfaction to me personally*". He was dismayed that earlier in 1929 work already done on the soundboards had to be re-done because of unusual 'atmospheric conditions'. This caused splits and warping of the wood resulting in air escaping unintentionally into other sections of the organ's mechanism causing extraneous noises when the pipes were replaced. It had been hoped to provide two consoles for the organ on the floor of the cathedral, one in the quire and one in the nave, but financial considerations prevented this. The single new console sat on the screen facing south between the two cases with the largest pedal pipes lying on the floor in a horizontal position, very close by, which Willis felt was far from ideal. He went on to describe in some detail the changes made during the re-building of the organ and these are summarised as follows.

The Great Organ was found to be unbalanced and weak in 4´ tone when set against the four 8´ Diapasons, each one of which was made by a different organ builder. The largest was very heavy toned and not part of the normal chorus structure. The second and third were very similar in style and construction to each other, so

Willis re-voiced them to contrast – the second being made more bold and third more cantabile in tone. He thought the very old pipes by Smith to be the most interesting but the pipes were in a sad condition and needed careful restoration. To rectify the problem of balance the Gamba was cut down to make an Octave No. 1, the Principal becoming Octave No 2. The whole department was re-voiced throughout. The 4´ Harmonic Flute was transferred to the choir and replaced by a stopped flute, formed from the old choir Gedackt 8´. The Mixture was re-cast to include the Twelfth (which had been removed in 1908), using the pipes of the Swell Mixture.

The Swell Organ was in a very disadvantageous position, sunken as it was within the arch in the bottom of the south case. So Willis took bold measures, re-voicing throughout on much higher wind pressures, which he felt was essential to project the tone into the building. He revoiced the Diapason and Octave to produce 'a more interesting tone colour' and the Mixture was from the old Great and suitably remodelled. The Swell-box was 'thicknessed up [sic] to obtain a proper crescendo and diminuendo'. Willis acknowledged that the effect on the Swell reeds of the heavy pressure, the muffling effect of a poor position and their natural harmonic structure due to their construction tended to make them sound more like Tubas in tone.

The Choir Organ was completely remodelled with all the stops enclosed in a swell-box, which was enlarged and again suitably thickened. The Open Diapason had to remain unenclosed because its bass pipes were on display in the South case. The remaining stops were either re-voiced or made out of other old stops. Three stops were transferred elsewhere (the 8´ Gedackt to the Great at 4´, the Corno-di-Bassetto moved to the Solo and Tunks' extremely small-scaled Viole pipes were moved to the Swell and cut down by an octave to make a Celeste). Willis provided two stops with new ranks of pipes: the 8´ Wald Flute with triangular treble pipes and the 2´ Piccolo, the old Swell Celeste pipes became the new Viole, the Flute Harmonique 4´ came from the Great and the Nazard and Tierce were made from converting the old 4´ and 2´ flutes respectively.

The Solo Organ's pipes were all re-voiced and even the Tuba was placed in the swell box, which had been enlarged accordingly, and re-voiced on a higher pressure of wind. The French Horn was declared to be 'utterly useless' and was accordingly scrapped and replaced by the Corno-di-Bassetto from the old Choir organ. Willis noted that the 'free reed' Cor Anglais pipes were made in France, and had a 'tendency towards wheeziness, reminiscent, naturally, of the harmonium'.

The Pedal Organ remained much as before but with two 4´ stops extended from the 8´ranks. Again all the stops were revoiced.

There were 52 speaking stops operated by drawstops, and 37 couplers, etc., operated by stop-tabs over the top manual, which was the 'Willis' house style. All the actions, including the swell pedals, were electro-pneumatic and all the pistons were adjustable from the keyboards. All the reeds were re-voiced in Willis's house style. The shutters of the swell boxes were made to open so that the sound was deflected towards the roof, in order to make as much as of their poor position. The Swell Organ's box could not be moved to a better position because no other space was available.

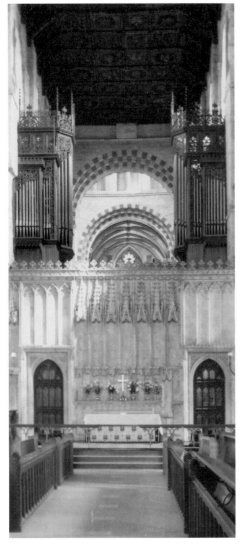

c.1950
The appearance of the organ from the nave, divided between J.O. Scott's two cases, remained unchanged from 1908 to 1959 (from the Cathedral Archives)

Specification of the organ as re-built by Willis (1929)

Great Organ
(13 stops, 9 couplers)

1	Double Open Diapason	16	R	Hill (bass pipes in north case)
2	Open Diapason No. 1*	8	R	Abbott and Smith (1908)
3	Open Diapason No. 2	8	R	Tunks (1921)
4	Open Diapason No. 3	8	R	Hill (bass pipes in north case)
5	Open Diapason No. 4	8	R	Smith (1670)
6	Stopped Diapason	8	R	Hill (stopped wood)
7	Octave No. 1	4	R	Hill old Gamba remade
8	Octave No. 2	4	R	Hill
9	Flute Couverte	4	PN	Hill old Choir 8' (stopped metal)
10	Fifteenth	2	R	Hill
11	Mixture 12,19, 22	3 rks	PN	Hill, old Swell Mixture remodelled
12	Tromba*	8	R	Abbott and Smith (1908)/Tunks (harmonic trebles - 1921)
13	Clarion*	4	R	Abbott and Smith (1908)/Tunks (harmonic trebles - 1921)

i	Swell to Great	vi	Choir to Great, 16´
ii	Swell to Great, 4´	vii	Solo to Great
iii	Swell to Great, 16´	viii	Solo to Great, 4´
iv	Choir to Great	ix	Solo to Great, 16´
v	Choir to Great, 4´		

Swell Organ (enclosed)
(13 stops, 4 couplers and 2 Tremolos).

14	Bordun	16	R	Hill (stopped wood)
15	Geigen Diapason	8	R	Hill
16	Lieblich Gedackt	8	R	Hill (stopped wood and metal)
17	Viola	8	R	Abbott and Smith (1908)
18	Voix Celestes (tenor C)	8	R	Tunks, (1921), old Choir Viole rescaled
19	Octave Geigen	4	R	Hill
20	Hohl Flute	4	R	Tunks (1921), former 8' transposed (wood)
21	Fifteenth	2	R	Hill
22	Mixture 15,19,22	3 rks	R	Hill, old Great Mixture
23	Waldhorn*	16	R	Hill
24	Trumpet *	8	R	Abbott and Smith (1908)/Tunks (harmonic trebles - 1921)
25	Oboe *	8	R	Hill
26	Clarion *	4	R	Abbott and Smith (1908)/Tunks (harmonic trebles - 1921)

x Swell Octave
xi Swell Sub-Octave
xii Swell Unison off
xiii Solo to Swell
xiv Tremolo (H.P.*)
xv Tremolo (L.P.)

* = H.P. – stops on the higher wind pressure
L.P. = stops on the lower wind pressure

Choir Organ (enclosed)

(10 stops, 9 couplers and Tremolo)

27	Open Diapason (unenclosed)	8	R	Abbott and Smith (1908 - pipes in south case)
28	Viole d'Orchestre	8	R	Abbott and Smith (1908), old Swell Celeste pipes
29	Dulciana	8	R	Abbott and Smith (1908)
30	Wald Flute	8	PN	Willis (wood) (old bass)
31	Gemshorn	4	R	Hill
32	Flute Harmonique	4	R	Hill
33	Nazard	2⅔	PN	Hill, old 4' Wald Flute pipes (wood)
34	Piccolo	2	N	Willis
35	Tierce	1⅗	PN	Hill, old 2' Flautina remodelled
36	Clarinet	8	R	Hill

xvi	Choir Octave	xxi	Swell to Choir, 16'
xvii	Choir Sub-Octave	xxii	Solo to Choir
xviii	Choir Unison off	xxiii	Solo to Choir, 4'
xix	Swell to Choir	xxiv	Solo to Choir, 16'
xx	Swell to Choir, 4'	xxv	Tremolo

Solo Organ (enclosed)

(6 stops, 3 couplers and Tremolo)

37	Doppel Flute	8	R	Abbott and Smith (1908) (wood)
38	Concert Flute	4	R	Abbott and Smith (1908)
39	Corno-di-Bassetto	16	R	Abbott and Smith (1908), formerly on the Choir
40	Orchestral Oboe	8	R	Abbott and Smith (1908)
41	Cor Anglais	8	R	Abbott and Smith (free reed) (1908)
42	Tuba*	8	R	Abbott and Smith (1908)/Tunks (harmonic trebles - 1921)

xxvi	Solo Octave	xxviii	Solo Unison off
xxvii	Solo Sub-Octave	xxix	Tremolo (L.P.)

Pedal Organ

(10 stops, 8 couplers)

43	Sub Bass	32	R	Abbott and Smith (stopped wood)
44	Resultant Bass (derived from 45)	32	R	Abbott and Smith / Hill (wood)
45	Open Diapason	16	R	Hill (wood)
46	Violone	16	R	Abbott and Smith (1885 – pipes in the south case)
47	Bourdon	16	R	Hill (stopped wood)
48	Octave	8	R	Hill (metal)
49	Bass Flute	8	R	Abbott and Smith (1908) (stopped wood)(partly from 47)
50	Super Octave	4	PN	Hill / Willis (partly from 48)
51	Octave Flute	4	PN	Hill / Abbott and Smith / Willis (stopped wood) (partly from 47 and 49)
52	Trombone*	16	PN	Hill (wood)

xxx Swell to Pedal	xxxiv Solo to Pedal
xxxi Swell to Pedal, 4′	xxxv Solo to Pedal, 4′
xxxii Choir to Pedal	xxxvi Great to Pedal
xxxiii Choir to Pedal, 4′	xxxvii Great and Pedal Combinations Coupled

R = remodelled and revoiced
PN = part new
N = new

Accessories

6 Pistons to Great Organ
6 Pistons to Swell Organ
6 Pistons to Choir Organ
6 Pistons to Solo Organ
6 Toe Pistons to Pedal Organ
(All instantly adjustable from the keyboards on the latest 'Willis' system)
6 'General Pistons' acting over all stops and couplers*
1 General Cancel Toe Piston
1 Pedal Cancel Piston
1 Cancel Piston on each Manual
1 Reversible Piston to Great to Pedal *
1 Reversible Piston to Swell to Great
1 Reversible Piston to Choir to Great
1 Reversible Piston to Solo to Great
1 Reversible Piston to Great and Pedal Combinations Coupled
1 Reversible Piston to Solo to Swell
1 Reversible Piston to Swell to Choir
1 Reversible Piston to Solo to Choir
1 Reversible Piston to Swell to Pedal
1 Reversible Piston to Solo to Pedal
1 Reversible Piston to Choir to Pedal
1 Locking Piston for adjustment of Pistons
1 'General Crescendo' by balanced pedal-with indicator

1 'Full Organ' by reversible toe piston-with indicator
Balanced Swell Pedals to Swell, Choir and Solo boxes with electro-pneumatic swell engines.
Detached Console

*Duplicated by toe pistons.

Compass for the manuals CC to C, 61 notes, and a 'Willis' pedal board, CCC to F, 30 notes

Wind pressures

Great: light wind, 4 inches; heavy wind, 7 inches
Swell: light wind, 6 inches; heavy wind, 12 inches
Choir: throughout, 4 ½ inches
Solo: light wind, 7 inches; Tuba, 12 inches
Pedal: Flue work, 7 inches; Trombone, 12 inches

CHAPTER 6

THE HARRISON & HARRISON ORGAN (1962)

Unfortunately the work done in 1929 fared only a little better and lasted slightly longer than the work done 20 years earlier. During the 1950s, successive faults began to show in the organ mechanism, and the wind supply became increasingly noisy.

After the Second World War there was also a major change in the awareness of other musical cultures. Gradually the more enlightened British organists were becoming interested in learning about the different sounds and styles of construction of organs in other European countries. They were discovering that the characteristic sounds of the organs from different national styles had in turn influenced and inspired the native composers. Organists had a new interest in the reproduction of sounds which were perceived to be more faithful and 'authentic', especially in the historic instruments of earlier centuries which seemed to have survived in greater abundance in mainland Europe than in England. The new generation of organists and organ builders was gradually coming to realize that the traditional English cathedral organ of the early twentieth century had definite musical limitations.

In the late 1950s four things came together in St Albans which together achieved a remarkable outcome. The first was inevitable dissatisfaction with the existing cathedral organ regarding its tonal output and musical impact in the building (the Willis rebuild having changed the sound only insomuch that it went from being muffled to a muffled roar) as well as its failing mechanical reliability. Second, there was the change in the kind of organ that was fashionable for the new generation of organists and the lovers of organ music. Third was the Dean's imaginative appointment of a brilliant new organist, Peter Hurford, who was young, energetic and rapidly gaining an international reputation as a specialist performer in stylish performances of Baroque organ music, and of J. S. Bach in particular. Finally, work began on the restoration of wall-paintings in the nave and on the repair of the immense area of plaster in the nave, choir and transepts. To facilitate repairs to the walls above and behind the organ cases it was decided that the organ was to be dismantled in September 1959. It was therefore agreed in 1958 that this was an ideal opportunity to start afresh with the organ, which would be entirely rebuilt, and 1962 was fixed as the year in which the new organ would be opened, by which time all the dusty work on the plaster would be complete.

Eventually a contract was placed with Messrs Harrison & Harrison of Durham and no other firm was invited to tender.[30] An independent consultant was appointed – Ralph Downes[31] – who had worked closely with Harrisons in the early 1950s when they built the Royal Festival Hall (RFH) organ to his design. Harrisons were seen as having the expertise to voice pipework (and especially the upper work) of greater clarity than other contemporary English organ builders. Hurford and Downes had become good friends and between them they exchanged ideas in order to reach the final specification for St Albans. Downes took a very personal hand in the scaling of the pipes and an ear in the voicing, having learned much from working on the RFH organ, while Hurford was

---

30 At that time there was no question of inviting a builder from mainland Europe: the 'English Cathedral Organ Tone' was seen as something that foreign builders would be unable to achieve.

31 Ralph Downes was organist of Brompton Oratory and it is an interesting coincidence that Mr Pitts – a predecessor of Mr Downes at the Oratory – played the Hill organ at the opening service in 1861.

The 1962 Choir Organ
case designed by Cecil Brown, the Abbey Surveyor
(photograph by Colin Pinchbeck, from the Cathedral Archives)

determined to have an organ that could not only accompany the cathedral services – both small and large – well, but also be reasonably authentic for most schools of organ music.

Fortunately, a little two manual organ of 13 speaking stops was available for hire between 1959 and 1962. Referred to as the 'Portable' organ, it had been built by Harrisons in 1957 for experimental purposes, undoubtedly with some input from Downes. It had been used at Westminster Abbey in 1958/59 during the time that the organ there was out of commission owing to repairs to the casework. It came straight from Westminster to St Albans Abbey in 1959, where it was erected in the centre of the nave screen, and was most successful in the accompaniment of services for three years. It was subsequently bought by Mr Arthur Starke and formed the basis of his house organ on the Isle of Wight.

Specification of the temporary organ, built by Harrison & Harrison in 1957
This stood in the centre of the nave screen from 1959 to 1962.

Great Organ (6 stops, 1 coupler)

1	Open Diapason*	8
2	Stopped Diapason	8
3	Principal	4
4	Spitzflute	4
5	Fifteenth	2
6	Mixture 19.22.26	III rks
	i Swell to Great	

(*added in 1958 for Westminster Abbey)

Swell Organ

7	Spitzflute	8
8	Quintadena	4
9	Gemshorn	2
10	Rauschterz 22.29 / 15.17	II rks

Composition of Rauschterz:

C-F# 7 notes 22.29
G-b 5 notes 22.26
c-f# 7 notes 22.24
g-c# 31 notes 17.22
d-c 11 notes 15.17

Pedal Organ (3 stops, 2 couplers)

11	Sub Bass	16
12	Octave	8
13	Waldflute	4
	ii Great to Pedal	
	iii Swell to Pedal	

Wind pressures:

Great: $2\frac{3}{8}$ inches
Swell and Pedal: $2\frac{5}{8}$ inches

Accessories
5 thumb pistons each to Great and Swell
5 toe pistons to Pedal
Reversible pistons to ii and i
Reversible toe piston to ii
Electro-pneumatic action.
Detached drawstop console.

Peter Hurford at the Harrison & Harrison organ. Note the position of the organ console in its original alignment
(photograph by Colin Pinchbeck, from the Cathedral Archives)

Construction in the Abbey of the rebuilt cathedral organ began immediately after Easter 1962, and the organ was dedicated by the Bishop of St Albans on 18 November.

The first question of design which had to be tackled was the internal disposition of the organ. Since 1908, the Great Organ had been level with the floor of the organ loft, while the Swell was buried in an arch in the south choir aisle, so that neither could be heard effectively from the nave. Furthermore, the entire organ loft (one of the largest in the country) had been occupied by the 32′ Sub Bass, 16′ Open Wood and 16′ Trombone laid horizontally.

It was decided that all the pipework should stand inside the two 1908 cases, which would be raised by 0.75 metres from the floor

of the loft in order to house the pipes of the Pedal 32′ Subbass in an upright position. This would also create more room in general for additional pipework. It was also proposed that a new Choir Organ case should be built to the design of Mr Cecil Brown, FRIBA, the Abbey Surveyor, thus leaving the organ loft clear of all obstruction, apart from the Choir Organ and console, and its free area of some 75 square metres would be available for a small orchestra or choir.

The Great Organ was placed at two levels high up in the south case, and the Swell in a similar position (also at two levels) in the north case. The Fanfare Trumpets sat above the Great, hooded to face west, and the Grand Cornet of five ranks was mounted in the central pipe-tower of the south case between the upper and lower levels. The Pedal Organ was divided between the two main cases at the lowest level, with the Principal chorus, 32′ Subbass and Quint in the North case and the remainder (reeds and flutes) in the South.

After much consideration, the designers also decided to dispense with the idea of a fourth manual division and allocated the money saved towards necessary extra pipework instead. The new organ had a total of 73 ranks (including mixture-work) compared with the previous organ's total of 52. Three stops were made available on more than one division of the organ, and there was no extension. The elegant new detached console on the screen had 71 stop-knobs contained in curved jambs.

Tonally, this organ was the first English cathedral organ to be voiced on the principle of open-foot voicing and relatively low wind-pressures. Justification for the designers' decision to adopt these principles was immediately apparent when the temporary organ was installed in 1959; it was found that the speech and tone of the pipes – especially when heard from the west end of the nave – produced a delicately clear sound which was both beautiful and effective in leading a large congregation. The organ's specification was designed to fulfil the very varied demands made upon it in the course of Cathedral and festival services as well as being suited to playing organ music from all the major periods of composition with appropriate registration.

In his autobiography *Baroque Tricks* Downes refers to his approach to his design at St Albans though he distances himself somewhat from the final overall result.[32] He was concerned with the adequate projection of tone down the building and describes one feature of the design meant to achieve this.[33] Other critics have acknowledged that this organ 'brought a more coherent classical sound to the centres of the established churches, and showed that classicism was not necessarily an enemy of choral accompaniment.'[34]

The completion of the organ in 1962 attracted much attention. In 1963 the Congress of the International Society of Organ Builders visited St Albans and was much interested by this new concept of organ design in an English cathedral. The same year saw the inauguration of an International Organ Festival which from the start proved an immediate success in providing a unique stimulus to young organists from England and indeed the world over. The Festival, which is still held in alternate years, welcomes distinguished organists of international standing as recitalists and competition judges, and has gained a worldwide reputation for the wide variety of its musical fare which consistently attracts large audiences. The organ proved highly successful in accompanying services and in its secondary role as a vivid recital instrument. It has inspired regular concerts every season, and has featured a great deal in recordings and on radio and television.

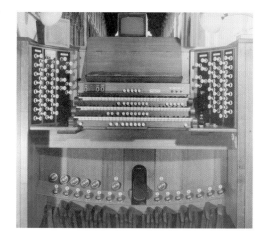

After 1973
The console of the Harrison & Harrison organ after it had been moved in 1973 to the centre of the screen, the player facing west (photograph from the Cathedral Archives)

---

32 *Baroque Tricks*, page 202: 'though over the voicing and finishing I had only a limited amount of control and therefore limited responsibility for the effect.'

33 i.e. the 'considerable spatial separation of all divisions, involving a difference of acoustic ambience between the screen area (Positive) [by which Downes means Choir] and the triforium level (Great and Swell) … a most important unifying principle was the ample scaling of the wide-open flutes – Pedal 16-feet, Great 8-feet, Swell 4-feet and Positive 2-feet.' He goes on to describe that 'this was a fact which has not always been perceptibly grasped by such players as habitually plan their registration visually or theoretically rather than aurally'.

34 Bicknell: *The History of the English Organ*, page 349.

Specification of the Harrison & Harrison Organ, 1962

(incorporating revisions made in 1973 and 1991)

H=Hill (10 stops, and part of 3 others); AS=Abbott and Smith (8 stops and part of 2 others); T=Tunks (part of 4 stops). All old pipes were revoiced. The remaining 31 stops were made by Harrison & Harrison. All pipes are spotted metal unless specified.

Great Organ (14 stops)

1	Principal	16	AS Violone bass 24 pipes, except low C #, in case; H Great 16' treble
2	Bourdon	16	new, stopped plain metal
3	Principal	8	AS Choir Open Diapason bass 10 pipes in case; remainder H Open Diapason III
4	Diapason	8	1-17 new, remainder AS.
5	Spitzflute	8	new, tapered
6	Stopped Diapason	8	new, stopped plain metal
7	Octave	4	new
8	Stopped Flute	4	new, stopped spotted metal with chimneys
9	Blockflute	2	new, plain metal
10	Quartane 12 15	II rks	12th rank new, 15th rank H rescaled
11	Mixture 19 22 26 29	IV-VI rks	new, repitched higher in 1973
12	Trumpet	16	H & T Swell Double Trumpet, new French shallots
13	Grand Cornet 1 8 12 15 17	V rks	from tenor g, new spotted metal, 8' stopped with chimneys, remainder open
14	Fanfare Trumpet	8	new, hooded, harmonic from treble c

Swell Organ (15 stops)

15	Open Diapason	8	H, rescaled
16	Rohrflute	8	new, plain metal, with chimneys from middle c
17	Viola	8	AS rescaled
18	Celeste	8	from tenor c, mostly H
19	Principal	4	H, rescaled
20	Open Flute	4	new, spotted metal
21	Nazard	2⅔	new, tapered plain metal
22	Gemshorn	2	new, tapered plain metal
23	Tierce	1⅗	new, tapered plain metal
24	Mixture 22 26 29	III rks	new 1991 replacing former Cimbel (1962, revised 1973)
25	Hautboy	8	H, caps removed, new French shallots from middle c
26	Vox Humana	8	new
27	Corno di Bassetto	16	AS (belled resonators) with new extension up to 70 notes
28	Trumpet	8	AS & T, new French shallots
29	Clarion	4	AS & T, new French shallots

1962
Inside the Choir Organ of the Harrison & Harrison organ (photograph by Colin Pinchbeck, from the Cathedral Archives)

Choir Organ (13 stops)

30	Quintaton	16	H Swell 16', bottom 12 pipes, wood; from tenor c new, stopped plain metal
31	Open Diapason	8	new, tapered spotted metal
32	Gedackt-pommer	8	new, bottom 24 pipes in the case
33	Flauto traverso	8	new, stopped plain metal
34	Octave	4	new
35	Rohrflute	4	new stopped plain metal with chimneys, treble spotted metal
36	Waldflute	2	new, tapered spotted metal
37	Larigot	1⅓	new, tapered spotted metal
38	Sesquialtera 19 24	II rks	new
39	Mixture 26 29 33 36	IV rks	new, repitched higher in 1973
40	Cromorne	8	H Clarinet, caps removed, new French shallots
41	Grand Cornet	V rks	duplicating Great No. 13
42	Fanfare Trumpet	8	duplicating Great No. 14

Pedal Organ (15 stops)

43	Sub Bass	32	AS, stopped wood
44	Principal	16	H old Great 16' bottom 24 pipes (except low C #) displayed in case
45	Majorbass	16	H, wood
46	Bourdon	16	H, stopped wood
47	Quint	10⅔	new, stopped; 5 zinc, remainder plain metal
48	Octave	8	H bass 10 pipes Great Open Diapason III in case, remainder T Open Diapason II
49	Gedackt	8	new, stopped plain metal
50	Nazard	5⅓	new, bass 12 pipes stopped plain metal, remainder tapered
51	Choral Bass	4	AS Great Open Diapason I, heavy metal
52	Open Flute	2	new, plain metal
53	Mixture 19 22 26 29	IV rks	new
54	Bombardon	16	H wood resonators, new French shallots
55	Trumpet	16	duplicating Great No. 12
56	Tromba	8	AS Solo Tuba, new French shallots
57	Shawm	4	AS Solo Orchestral Oboe

Couplers

Choir to Pedal +
Great to Pedal + #
Swell to Pedal +
Choir Tremulant
Choir Octave
    (did not affect stop 41)
Choir Unison Off
    (did not affect stops 41 and 42)
Swell to Choir +
Choir to Great +
    (did not affect stops 41 and 42)
Swell to Great + #
Swell Tremulant
Swell Octave
Swell Sub-Octave
Swell Unison Off
Great and Pedal Combinations Coupled

Accessories

7 thumb pistons to the Great
6 thumb pistons to the Choir
7 thumb pistons to the Swell
    (duplicated by toe pistons)
7 toe pistons to the Pedal
5 General thumb pistons (increased to 10 in 1973)
    (1–5 duplicated by toe pistons)
General Cancel
Setter Piston
Reversible thumb pistons to couplers marked +
    Reversible toe pistons to couplers marked #
Memory levels: 160 for General pistons (2001)
    and 8 for Divisional pistons (1989)
Balanced Swell pedal (mechanical)
Manual compass CC–a, 58 notes;
Pedal compass CCC–G, 32 notes

Wind Pressures

Great: 3⅝ inches; Fanfare Trumpet, 7½ inches
Swell: 3⅝ inches
Choir: 2⅝ inches
Pedal: 4 inches

During the summer of 1972, the nave of the cathedral was considerably remodelled to cope with present day liturgical needs and to provide sorely needed additional seating. This work created a great deal of dust and accordingly, it was decided to advance the date for the organ cleaning planned for 1974, to the winter of 1972/73. While the organ was stripped down, the manual mixtures were slightly raised in pitch and the number of general pistons was increased from five to ten. The advent of closed-circuit television and sound equipment meant that the console could be moved to the centre of the screen, with the organist facing west,[35] which increased the amount of usable space in the loft and gave the organist a truer sense of the balance of the organ's divisions.

Over the next 15 years more repairs to the Cathedral fabric made a further cleaning of the organ necessary in 1989, when the opportunity was taken to replace the original coupler and combination systems with solid-state electronic equipment. This gave more flexibility for storing registrations, particularly during the biennial International Organ Festival (IOF) competitions, on 32 memory levels for the ten general pistons, and eight levels for the divisional pistons.[36] The Swell Cimbel, as revised in 1973, had always proved itself a stop more to be avoided than used, so in 1991 it was replaced by a new lower pitched three-rank Mixture.

---

[35] In 1962, the necessity for the organist to see the nave and choir through mirrors meant that the console had to be placed obliquely to the line of the nave.

[36] In 2001, through the generosity of the Williams Church Music Trust, the number of memory levels for the general pistons was further increased to 160, specifically to make life easier for all performers during the period of the Festival.

CHAPTER 7

THE ORGAN INTO THE TWENTY-FIRST CENTURY – RESTORING THE HARRISON & HARRISON ORGAN (2007–9)

The Harrison & Harrison organ has stood the test of time and given excellent service in the daily round of cathedral worship and in hundreds of concerts and recitals. It is remarkably versatile and has proved to be extremely rewarding for the player who aims to make music.

2009
The Choir Organ with Cimbelstern (photograph by David Kelsall)

But to the thoughtless or musically unprepared player it can be utterly unforgiving and it will never flatter or disguise a poorly conceived performance.

After almost trouble-free service for over forty years it became clear that the organ was starting to show its age – there were signs of wear and tear, first of all with the key actions seeming less responsive than they had been, with the occasional note ceasing to function altogether, and increasingly noisy wind leaks from the pneumatic part of the stop actions.

More disturbingly, the level of heating in the cathedral in the winter had been kinder to people than it was to the organ, causing excessive drying out of the organ's mechanisms. A series of unexpected problems with the functioning of the organ's humidifier revealed that the organ had actually been relying on the humidifier to keep it playable during the winter months. For several consecutive years, in the busy run-up to Christmas, some of the most used stops for accompaniment would cease to function and sounds emanated unbidden from some of the smaller pipes – clear signs of the need for restoration.

So in the last few months of the twentieth century the Cathedral Chapter requested that a fresh assessment be made of the organ's condition in order that they might plan for the future. Reports were invited from the organ builder, the Master of the Music and from Ian Bell, the Chapter's independent organ consultant. These confirmed that, while all was still in quite good order and that the organ was remarkably reliable for its age, the relatively dry atmosphere in the cathedral was speeding up the ageing process in the organ's action, with serious splits becoming more common in the leather stop motors and movement in various wooden parts of the action and soundboards.

The Chapter supported the Master of the Music's view that the organ is crucial to the continued programme of choral music in the worship in the cathedral, and that it is also important to the Cathedral that it should continue to be the instrument at the heart of the biennial International Organ Festival (IOF).

Therefore retaining an instrument upon which players may perform to the highest standard, whether in service or concert, was a priority. A plan emerged whereby the organ could be restored between two consecutive Organ Festivals and the process of consultation and fund raising began in 2001. Ian Bell was retained as consultant to the Dean and Chapter and, with Andrew Lucas as the artistic adviser for the project, plans were drawn for the revision of the specification.

Two organ builders were invited to submit their proposals for the full restoration of the instrument, the intention being that the organ should last for at least the next 50 or 60 years, and hopefully for much longer, with minimal intervention other than routine maintenance. It was a requirement that the organ's mechanisms should return to a condition as if new and that the instrument should be robust enough to resist damage from any periods of extreme dryness and low humidity in the cathedral.

A decision was taken to renew the soundboards and replace any parts of the action that could not be expected to last for a significantly long time. It was also deemed prudent that the wind reservoirs, should be fully restored and re-leathered, thus avoiding the expense of a full dismantling of the organ again in the near future. Harrison & Harrison again emerged as the organ-builder best placed to take the organ forward into the next generation – their intimate knowledge of the instrument over the first 45 years of its life in its current form being seen as a distinct advantage.

When the organ was originally designed a number of compromises were made owing to various limitations, including the availability of funds. This helped define the character of the instrument, but inevitably some compromises have proved less happy than others. Part of the latest work has been to address these compromises and, where possible, eliminate them. The chief areas of concern rested on Downes' curious avoidance of Principal stops at 2′ pitch, which was a particular handicap in the Swell where such a stop would be helpful in the build-up of the Swell chorus in choral accompaniment. Also although the Swell Mixture was an improvement it had been voiced with a bias towards retaining the classical balance between the manual choruses. The result was therefore still somewhat intrusive in the context of choral accompaniment. The lack of Great reeds at 8´ and 4´ pitch always left the tutti feeling less than complete, yet the addition of the Fanfare Trumpet (rather hopefully intended to fulfil a dual chorus and solo rôle) was never satisfactory, especially when heard from the nave where its bright tone is particularly directional. Finally, in such a large building the tutti needed more gravitas of the sort that only 32´ reed pipes provide. It had been hoped that room could be found for such a stop in the 1960s, but in the end it was thought to be impossible to house the pipes within the organ cases.

The great length of St Albans Cathedral (one of the longest mediaeval naves in Britain) means that the organ has to work very hard when the building is full to have presence in the westernmost half of the nave – someone sitting there feels that the organ sounds very distant and hymn singing is less well supported than one would hope. Consideration was therefore given to the provision of a small chorus of stops and a pedal 16´ bass, with additional flute ranks at 8´ and 4´ for quieter support, which would give that sense that the organ is nearer and more supportive to the congregation.

All the actions have been renewed and leather work replaced with new. The electrical systems have been totally replaced while the soundboard grids have been restored and the tables and sliders replaced with new. The two pedal soundboards turned out to have been re-used manual soundboards from the old organ and, being considered unsuitable for further restoration, have been replaced with new. The old electro-pneumatic slider actions, which proved to be intrusively noisy in operation, have been replaced by modern slider solenoids which are almost silent in operation.

2009
The north case (photograph by David Kelsall)

All the pipework has been restored and the style of this organ has been retained scrupulously – the flue stops are still regulated at the mouth and none of the pipes are nicked. The regulation of pipes voiced in this way is a very sensitive process, but it was felt important not to change the style of voicing when working on these pipes. The manual Mixture stops, which had all been altered, have been returned to their original form. Any changes have been done discreetly and additions considered carefully in the light of the general style and ethos of the instrument. The two constituent ranks of the Great Quartane have been made available separately, increasing the possibilities for more subtle registrations, whilst the pipes of the Grand Cornet, which were tightly packed in a relatively low position in the central tower, now sing out from a commanding position at the top of the tower. Adjacent to the Cornet but slightly below sit the new Great chorus reeds, made in the same style as the existing 16´ stop.

The Swell has also gained its much needed 2′ Octave and the Mixture of 1991 has been retained, but re-voiced to blend more successfully – the need for a sharper pitched stop is answered by the insertion of a new Cimbel at the same pitch as the original from 1962. The mutation ranks are now affected by the Tremulant.

The new small Solo division has just one stop of its own – the Fanfare Trumpet. With the advent of new Great chorus reeds at 8′and 4′, this stop has been released from its former somewhat compromised rôle as both the climax stop for the Great and as a solo voice on the Choir manual. Consequently it has been revoiced with new tongues and on a slightly higher wind pressure to give it a broader and stronger sonority. The Solo also has duplications of the Great Organ's Grand Cornet and the Corno-di-Bassetto from the Swell, as well as the ability to transfer the Great reeds to this keyboard. From these quite slender resources (and the octave coupler) there is considerable scope for additional colourful registrations and flexibility in both the written repertoire and in improvisations.

The Pedal Organ has received a much longed-for 32′reed stop, with full length resonators situated within the south case. Care has been taken to ensure that it balances the rest of the organ. This stop is also extended to 16′ pitch to provide a mezzo-forte reed stop which blends with the flue chorus by virtue of its rounder tone, positioned as it is with the other pedal stops in the base of the south case.

It was consideration of the future addition of a Nave Organ that finally effected a late revision to the contract for a new four manual console. It was realised that, with the installation of the Nave Organ, it would be rather complex and musically restricting to control three very different divisions from one keyboard. So the Choir Organ now has a manual keyboard to itself, the three stop Solo division shares the additional fourth manual with the Nave Organ.

2009
The south organ
case with
Andrew Lucas
at the console
(photograph by
David Kelsall)

The new console preserves the distinctive style and appearance of the original, especially with its curved stop jambs, though the wood is stained a deeper shade to match the organ casework rather than retaining the original light oak colour from before. The console position has been reversed so that the player now faces east, which achieves a happier sense of balance between the divisions. The bulk of the console shields the player from the pipes nearest to the console with the benefit of a greater sense of the nave's resonant acoustic. Modern piston control systems have been added and players can now luxuriate in a plethora of conveniently placed stepper pistons to operate the General pistons sequentially.

Finally, the opportunity was taken to make improvements to the appearance of the organ. Many of the old north and south case pipes in the east and west faces dating from 1861 and 1888, did not sound. The tarnished appearance and mismatch between pipe length and diameter, combined with less than satisfactory mouth lines and dry and damaged wood in the cases, gave the organ a tired and undistinguished profile. All the pipes on display in the north and south cases have been replaced with new ones of bright spotted metal, and the majority now speak. This has a dramatic effect on the instrument's appearance, and has also created more room inside the organ for better access, as well as allowing sufficient space for the 32′ reed pipes. Scott's cases have been cleaned and repaired and the expanded metal grilles have been replaced with more elegantly framed ones. Newly made linen-fold panels, matching existing ones on the east side, complete the west faces. The Choir Organ case has been fitted with electrically operated shutters to the west side, enabling the organist to focus the sound more directly into the quire or nave as required. The shutters close automatically when the organ is turned off, which means that the west window of the nave no longer shines through the front pipes of the Choir case when viewed from the east. A Cimbelstern (a rotating star with six bells) has been added to the upper flat of the Choir Organ case to a design based on carving to be found above the Canons' stalls on the north side of the quire.

Work commenced on the dismantling of the organ immediately after the IOF ended in the summer of 2007. Exactly one year later the first shipment returned from the organ works in Durham, the work of installation, voicing and regulation being completed ready for the services on Easter Day, 2009. With all the work and enhancements to the organ in this most recent restoration, the intention of the Chapter and the Master of the Music has been to preserve the sound of a successful musical instrument so that people will continue to be uplifted by the music that it makes. It is expected that the very thorough nature of the work will mean that the Cathedral and wider community will not need to face financing such thorough-going work for many decades to come and we hope that the instrument will inspire future generations, just as it has continued to do since its installation in 1962.

Specification of the Organ as rebuilt and restored by Harrison & Harrison, 2007–9

Great Organ (16 stops and 3 couplers)

1	Principal	16	new spotted metal bass in the case front
2	Bourdon	16	
3	Principal	8	new spotted metal bass in the case front
4	Diapason	8	new spotted metal bass in the case front
5	Spitzflute	8	
6	Stopped Diapason	8	
7	Octave	4	
8	Stopped Flute	4	
9	Quint	2⅔	from old Quartane
10	Super Octave	2	from old Quartane
11	Blockflute	2	
12	Mixture 19 22 26 29	IV-VI	restored to original composition
13	Bass Trumpet	16	
14	Trumpet	8	new, French shallots, harmonic from treble c
15	Clarion	4	new, French shallots, harmonic from middle c
16	Grand Cornet 1 8 12 15 17	V	from tenor g
i	Choir to Great		
ii	Swell to Great		
iii	Solo to Great		new coupler

Swell Organ (17 stops, Tremulant and 3 couplers)

17	Open Diapason	8	
18	Rohrflute	8	
19	Viola	8	
20	Celeste	8	from tenor c
21	Principal	4	
22	Open Flute	4	
23	Nazard	2⅔	
24	Octave	2	new addition
25	Gemshorn	2	
26	Tierce	1⅗	
27	Mixture 22 26 29	III	rebalanced
28	Cimbel 29 33 36	III	new, based on 1962 composition
29	Hautboy	8	
30	Vox Humana	8	
31	Corno di Bassetto	16	
32	Trumpet	8	
33	Clarion	4	
iv	Tremulant		
v	Octave		
vi	Sub-Octave		(not affecting no. 31)
vii	Unison Off		

Choir Organ (11 stops, Tremulant and 4 couplers)

34	Quintaton	16	
35	Open Diapason	8	
36	Gedackt-pommer	8	
37	Flauto traverso	8	
38	Octave	4	
39	Rohrflute	4	
40	Waldflute	2	
41	Larigot	1⅓	
42	Sesquialtera 19 24	II	
43	Mixture 22 26 29 33	IV	restored to original composition
44	Cromorne	8	
viii	Tremulant		
ix	Octave		
x	Unison Off		
xi	Swell to Choir		
xii	Solo to Choir		new coupler

Solo Organ (3 stops, Cimbelstern and 3 couplers)

45	Corno di Bassetto *Swell*	16	new addition, duplexed from no. 31
46	Grand Cornet *Great*	V	duplexed from 16 (formerly on the Choir)
47	Fanfare Trumpet	8	from Great, revoiced with new tongues, higher wind pressure
xiii	Octave		new coupler
xiv	Unison Off		
xv	Great Reeds on Solo		new coupler
48	Cimbelstern		new, 6 bells (untuned) and rotating star

Pedal Organ (17 stops and 4 couplers)

49	Sub Bass	32	
50	Principal	16	new spotted metal bass in the case front
51	Majorbass	16	
52	Bourdon	16	
53	Quint	10⅔	
54	Octave	8	new spotted metal bass in the case front
55	Gedackt	8	
56	Nazard	5⅓	
57	Choral Bass	4	
58	Open Flute	2	
59	Mixture 19 22 26 29	IV	
60	Fagotto	32	new addition, bass wood shallots with zinc resonators
61	Bombardon	16	
62	Fagotto	16	new addition, extended from no.60, trebles of spotted metal
63	Bass Trumpet *Great*	16	duplexed from no. 13
64	Tromba	8	
65	Shawm	4	
xvi	Choir to Pedal		
xvii	Great to Pedal		
xviii	Swell to Pedal		
xix	Solo to Pedal		new coupler

Nave Organ‡ (8 stops and 2 couplers)

66	Bourdon	16	bass 12 notes common with no. 73
67	Diapason	8	
68	Rohrflute	8	
69	Octave	4	
70	Spitzflute	4	
71	Super Octave	2	
72	Mixture 19 22 26 29	IV	
73	Pedal Subbass	16	
xx	Nave on Great *		
xxi	Nave on Solo		

Combination couplers

  xxii Great and Pedal Combinations Coupled

  xxiii Generals on Toe Pistons (1–8 on Swell, 9–16 on Pedal)

‡ prepared for in 2009 – to be installed at a later date

*coupler xx also allows the Nave stops to be set on the Great pistons

Accessories

Eight thumb pistons and cancel to Choir

Eight thumb pistons and cancel to Great

Eight thumb pistons and cancel to Swell

Three thumb pistons and cancel to Solo

Four thumb pistons and cancel to Nave

Sixteen General thumb pistons

Nine advance stepper pistons †

Two reverse stepper pistons †

General Cancel piston

Setter piston

Reversible thumb pistons to couplers:

i, ii, iii, xi, xv, xvi, xvii, xviii, xix, xx, xxi

Eight toe pistons to Pedal

Eight toe pistons duplicating the Swell thumb pistons

Two stepper advance toe pistons †

One stepper reverse toe piston †

Reversible toe pistons to couplers: xvii, xx

Reversible toe pedal to Cimbelstern

Balanced Swell Pedal (mechanical)

(† operating the General pistons in sequential order)

There are 8 levels of memory for the Divisional pistons, adjusted by rotary switch, and 256 levels for the General pistons, adjusted by a digital display. All piston levels are lockable with a key.

The manual compass is CC–a, 58 notes; and the pedalboard compass is CCC–G, 32 notes

Wind Pressures

Great: 3⅝ inches;

Swell: 3⅝ inches;

Choir: 2⅝ inches;

Solo: Fanfare Trumpet, 9 inches;

Pedal: 4 inches; Fagotto rank, 6 inches

Two Discus blowers for the main organ; one supplies the majority of the organ with wind while the second is a high pressure blower feeding the Fanfare Trumpet and Fagotto ranks only.

Mixture compositions (1962 and 2009)

Great Grand Cornet V (1962)

from tenor G	1	8	12	15	17

Great Mixture IV–VI
(restored to1962 pitch in 2009)

C	19	22	26	29		
tenor c	15	19	22	22	26	
middle c	12	15	15	19	22	22
middle f	8	12	15	15	19	22
treble c	8	8	12	15	15	19
treble a	8	8	12	12	15	15

Choir Sesquialtera II (1962)

C	19	24
tenor c	12	17

Choir Mixture IV
(restored to1962 pitch in 2009)

C	22	26	29	33
tenor c	19	22	26	29
tenor g	15	19	22	26
middle f	12	15	19	22
treble f	8	12	15	19
top c	8	8	12	15

Pedal Mixture IV (1962)

CC	19	22	26	29

Swell Mixture III
(1991, rebalanced 2009)

C	22	26	29
tenor c	19	22	26
middle c	15	19	22
treble c	12	15	19
top d#	8	12	15

Swell Cimbel III
(new 2009, based on 1962 Cimbel)

C	29	33	36
tenor c	22	29	33
tenor g	22	26	29
middle c	15	22	26
middle f	15	19	22
treble f#	12	15	19
top c# *	8	12	15

* in 1962 the last break was at top d#

Mixture compositions 1973 revisions

Great Mixture IV–VI

C	19	22	26	29		
tenor c	15	19	22	26	29	
middle c	12	15	19	22	26	
middle f	8	12	15	19	22	26
treble c	8	12	15	19	19	22
treble a	8	12	12	15	15	19
top d#	5	8	12	12	15	15

Choir Mixture IV

C	26	29	33	36
tenor c	22	26	29	33
tenor a#	19	22	26	29
middle a	15	19	22	26
treble g#	12	15	19	22
top d#	8	12	15	19

Swell Cimbel III

C	36	38	40
G	33	36	38
tenor c	31	33	36
tenor f	29	31	33
tenor a	26	29	31
middle c#	24	26	29
middle f#	22	24	26
middle a#	19	22	24
treble d	17	19	22
treble g	15	17	19
treble b	12	15	17
top d#	10	12	15

N.B. English Mixture pitches translated into feet (European notation):

$1 = 8$	$17 = 1\frac{3}{5}$	$31 = \frac{2}{5}$
$5 = 5\frac{1}{3}$	$19 = 1\frac{1}{3}$	$33 = \frac{1}{3}$
$8 = 4$	$22 = 1$	$36 = \frac{1}{4}$
$12 = 2\frac{2}{3}$	$24 = \frac{4}{5}$	$38 = \frac{1}{5}$
$15 = 2$	$26 = \frac{2}{3}$	$40 = \frac{1}{6}$
	$29 = \frac{1}{2}$	

CHAPTER 8
OTHER ORGANS IN THE CATHEDRAL

The organ in the Lady Chapel

In mediaeval times there were organs in the Lady Chapel, at the easternmost end of the Abbey Church, which were played during the daily Mass of Our Lady, music also being provided by the equivalent of the choir of boys who make up the current Cathedral Choir.

Today the Lady Chapel is still an important area for worship during the week – the majority of all wedding and funeral services take place in this beautiful space. The pipe organ currently standing at the west end of the chapel on the north side is most likely to be based upon a small one-manual instrument built in the late nineteenth/early twentieth century by Alfred Kirkland of Holloway in North London. It originally consisted of the following stops:

Manual (CC– g, 56 notes)

Open Diapason	8
Dulciana	8
[Gedeckt	8]
Harmonic Flute	4

Pedal (CCC–F, 30 notes)

Bourdon	16

Manual to Pedal coupler

The Lady Chapel Organ (photograph by David Kelsall)

Blowing was by hand and there was a trigger swell pedal and a radiating and concave pedalboard. The manual key action was mechanical and the pedal pneumatic.

In 1971 the organ builder Peter Collins, then of Redbourn (about 5 miles outside St Albans), remodelled the organ, adding an elegant new case to the front using burnished tin pipes for the bass of the 4′ stop, but utilizing some of the old pipes and the soundboard and key and stop actions. The revised specification is:

Manual (CC– g, 56 notes)

Wood Gedact	8	Old revoiced
Principal	4	New
Blockflute	2	Old 4′ flute remodelled
Mixture (19,22)	2 ranks	New

Pedal (CCC–F, 30 notes)

Bourdon	16	Old pipes, bottom 12 pipes only, remainder derived from 8′

Manual to Pedal coupler

A Discus electric blower was fitted. The pedal stop treble is derived from the bass of the 8′ stop by pneumatic action. Currently (2009) the soundboards and key actions are in a poor state of repair and require thorough repair or total replacement. Consequently the organ has not been in use for several years, although it remains in situ. It is hoped that the instrument will be restored at some time in the future.

Since the mid 1990s an Allen electronic substitute instrument has been in permanent use in the chapel, which has proved to be both musically versatile and mechanically reliable.

The Rendell Box Organ

Built by Peter Collins in 1984 and donated in memory of Robert Rendell, a former Cathedral Warden, this box organ is in used for small scale services, as an alternative accompanying instrument for verse anthems and as a continuo instrument in orchestral music. Collins built many similar organs including ones for hire from the builder's workshop, for private residences and for cathedrals, churches and chapels throughout the UK. It has become an invaluable resource for the cathedral musicians and is in frequent use. In 2008, after 24 years of use it was thoroughly overhauled and restored by Vincent Woodstock (also of Redbourn). It has a separate external electric blower unit and is mounted on castors for ease of movement around the building.

Specification (CC–d, 51 notes)

Wood Gedact	8
Rohr Flute	4
Principal	2

The dimensions of the organ are: 0.9m. x 1.04m. x 0.53m. The organ is housed in an oak case with a fretted ornamental pipeshade to the front, and removable doors which both protect the pipework and provides a means of controlling the volume of the organ. The note action is a simple mechanical (sticker) action and the stops are operated by slider controls at the left hand end of the keyboard. The action can be moved internally to enable the instrument to be played at a lower pitch, if required.

The Rendell Organ (photograph by David Kelsall)

The Rendell Organ (photograph by Alan Herbert)

International Organ Festival — temporary organs

A feature of the biennial St Albans International Organ Festival has been the importation of small organs which display the work of organ builders, great and small, and from both the UK and elsewhere in Europe.

For a period in the 1960s to 1980s slightly larger mechanical action organs were erected in the nave with the principal aim of being able to test the skill of competitors in the Organ Competitions in dealing with smaller instruments and sensitive mechanical action in appropriate repertoire. As an example of the type of instrument which was installed, the specification of an organ provided by D. A. Flentrop from Zaandam in The Netherlands which stood in the nave for the duration of the 1969 IOF is given below.

Manual I (CC–g, 56 notes)		Pedal (CCC–G, 32 notes)	
Roerfluit	8	Subbass	16
Prestant	4	Gedekt	8
Gemshoorn	2	Roerfluit	4
Mixtuur	III	Fagot	16
Kromhoorn	8		

Manual II (CC–g, 56 notes)		Couplers	
Gedekt	8	Manual I to Pedal	
Koppelfluit	4	Manual II to Pedal	
Prestant	2	Manual II to Manual I	
Quint	1 ⅓		
Sexquialter	II		
Tremulant			

CHAPTER 9
MUSICIANS AND ORGANISTS OF ST ALBANS ABBEY AND CATHEDRAL, 1302 TO THE PRESENT DAY

Musicians and organists in the monastery church of Saint Albans Abbey (1302–1539)

In 793 King Offa of Mercia founded a Benedictine monastery on the site of the martyrdom of St Alban, Britain's first recorded Christian martyr. After the Norman Conquest a new Abbey Church was started in 1077 and monastic life flourished until 5 December 1539 when the monastery was dissolved by King Henry VIII. Musicians, including some early organists, are mentioned in the accounts of the monastery from time to time and are listed below.

Adam, c.1302

Two organists, 1423

Robert Fayrfax, c.1498–1502 (b. Deeping Gate, Lincolnshire, 23 April 1464; d. 24 October 1521, aged 57).

Fayrfax held many high appointments – as a singer he is first recorded in 1500 among the lay clerks at the funeral of Prince Edmund, the third son of Henry VII. He was also present at the funeral of Queen Elizabeth, wife of Henry VII, on 23 February 1503, at the head of the singing men at the funeral of Henry VII (11 May 1509), the coronation of Henry VIII (24 June 1509), the funeral of Prince Henry (27 February 1511), and in the same rôle in 1520 he accompanied Henry VIII to the Field of the Cloth of Gold.

That Fayrfax requested that he be buried in the Presbytery of St Albans Abbey suggests that his connection with the Abbey must have been a substantial one. It has always been assumed the he was an organist of the Abbey, although his actual position is not entirely certain. His gravestone is now marked by an early twentieth century reproduction of a seventeenth-century rubbing of the monument brass which originally marked his tomb in the Abbey.

Anthony à Wood, the seventeenth century historian, says that in his day *'he was in great renowne and accounted the prime musitian of the nation'*. Three of his surviving works (*Salve regina*, *Regali Magnificat*, and the incomplete *Ave lumen gratiae*) are contained in the Eton Choirbook. His *Missa Albanus* received one of its earliest modern performances in St Albans Cathedral on 30 October, 1921 at the celebration of the 400th Anniversary of Fayrfax's death in a modified version, with the English text from the Book of Common Prayer, by W. L. Luttman.

Henry Besteney, 1529 is described as organist in a document of 1529. At the dissolution of the monastery in 1539 he received a pension of two marks a year and his board.

Organists of the Parish Church of St Albans Abbey (1821–1877)

After the Dissolution in 1539 the great Abbey church was left unused until 1553. It was saved by the people of the parish of St Andrew's, St Albans who bought it for £400 for use as their parish church (previously the Parish had worshipped in St Andrew's Chapel, which was attached to the north-west aisle of the nave). No organ is recorded as being in use in this period until 1821.

Thomas Fowler, 1821–31 was the first organist appointed when the Smith/Byfield/Gray organ was installed in the north transept in 1821. He resigned in 1831.

Edwin Theodore Alonzo Alphonso Don Carlos Nichols, 1831–33 (d. 1863). His Spanish names are accounted for by his mother being of Spanish extraction

Thomas Fowler, 1833–37 was re-appointed on the resignation of E.T.A.A.D.C. Nichols, but it is said that he absconded in 1837. He was so upset when he returned and found that the post had been filled in his absence that he died by his own hand.

Thomas Brooks, 1837–46

John Brooks, 1846–55
– was the brother of Thomas Brooks.

William Simmonds, 1855–1858.
Straker's history lists that Simmonds came to St Albans from Salisbury Cathedral, but he is not listed as one of the organists of that cathedral.

John Stocks Booth, 1858–79
(b. Sheffield, 1828; d. St Albans, 7 December 1879) was a pupil of Gaundett, Thalberg, Sterndale Bennett, and Molique. He was organist of Queen Street Chapel, Sheffield and then of Wortley Parish Church, near Sheffield, together with St Philip's, Sheffield. It was shortly after moving to Watford that he was appointed to St Albans Abbey in 1858. He is buried in the churchyard.

At the time of his appointment in 1858, the services were still of the old-fashioned parochial type, with metrical psalms from the Tate and Brady collection and a parish clerk. By the time of his death in 1879 a substantial choir of men and boys had been established.

Organists of St Albans Cathedral (1877–1957)

In 1877 the Parish Church of St Albans Abbey also became the Cathedral Church of the Diocese of St Albans when a new diocese was formed out of the Diocese of Rochester. The Rector at the time became the first Dean and the organist found himself elevated to the status of Cathedral organist.

John Stocks Booth became the first cathedral organist in 1877, until his death in 1879.

George Gaffe, 1880–1907

(b. Cawston, Norfolk, 27 July 1849; d. St Albans, September 1907). In the Herts Advertiser, 19 January 1907 we learn that:

'Mr George Gaffe FRCO who has held the position of organist & choirmaster of St Albans Cathedral since 1880 – a period of twenty-seven years – has placed his resignation in the hands of the Dean, as Rector, on account of ill-health and will relinquish his office after February.

Mr Gaffe, who was born in Cawston, Norfolk in 1849 entered Norwich Cathedral Choir as a probationer in 1857 and in the following year was made a full chorister. His love for music left to his being articled in 1862 to Dr Zachariah Buck, the well known organist of Norwich Cathedral for a term of seven years. Such promise did he show in his profession that he was appointed assistant organist and retained that office until 1874 when he obtained the post of organist at the Parish Church, Oswestry where he was associated with Henry Leslie in important festivals. Here he remained until 1880 when he applied for and secured the appointment of Organist at St Albans Cathedral in succession to Mr J S Booth. At that time the choir consisted of fourteen men and eighteen boys; whereas at the present time the men have increased to eighteen and there are six boy probationers. Under Mr Gaffe's regime the musical services have undergone striking changes. The introduction of a weekly Choral Service during the last ten years has been the most important development.

Apart from his connection with the Cathedral, Mr Gaffe has been prominently associated with the music of the city. He was responsible for starting the St Albans School of Music as a private venture in 1887 but its management later on was transferred to a committee and it has since been used as one of the public institutions for the city. For some years Mr Gaffe conducted a Choral Class in connection with the school and a number of works of the best composers were given. It was the practice to give two concerts a year in St Albans; but in consequence of lack of support and an accompanying lack of funds, the idea was abandoned. Mr Gaffe still holds the position of Principal of the School. Public recognition of his capacity as an organist was made in his appointment on the committee of the Royal College of Organists of which he is a fellow.'

And later that year, in September, the Herts Advertiser gave notice of Gaffe's death:

'Death of George Gaffe, FRCO, late organist of St Albans Cathedral aged 58 years. He was buried on 21st September 1907 in St Albans Cemetery. The body was taken to the Cathedral and was met at the great west door by the Very Reverend the Dean, the Reverend Alan Chaplin MA & the choir. The Psalm 39 was chanted and the hymns 'God moves in a mysterious way', and 'Peace, perfect peace' were sung. The only mourners were Dr and Mrs Mann[37], Mr Winor[38] of Stevenage & Mrs Giddens.'

Willie Lewis Luttman, 1907–30

(b. 20 February 1874; d. 2 February 1930)

The Herts Advertiser for 9 February 1907 announced that:

'As successor to Mr George Gaffe FRCO, Mr W L Luttman MA, Mus. Bac., Organist at the Parish Church Banbury has been appointed and will commence his duties at St Albans shortly after Easter. Mr Luttman who is an MA of Peterhouse, Cambridge has been organist at Banbury for the past nine years. His qualifications both as organist and choirmaster are highly spoken of. He has in fact brought the choir at Banbury to such a state of perfection that for two years in succession they have been successful competitors in the Choral Competitions open to the Choirs of the three counties Berks, Bucks, and Oxon.

Mr Luttman studied at the Royal College of Music, Kensington Gore under Sir Hubert Parry, Sir Frederick Bridge, Dr Gladstone, Dr Charles Higgs, Dr Charles Wood & others. He was "proxime accessit" for the organ scholarship and won an exhibition value £20, the adjudicators being M. Alexandre Guilmant, Sir Walter Parratt and Sir [Charles] Villiers Stanford. From Kensington he went to Peterhouse, Cambridge and proceeded to the MA degree taking afterwards that of MusBac. He is also an associate of the Royal College of Music and Fellow of the Royal College of Organists.'

---

37 Dr A. H. (Daddy) Mann was a fellow chorister of Zachariah Buck at Norwich and became the organist of King's College, Cambridge. It was in Mann's time there that the Festival of Lessons and Carols on Christmas Eve became established.

38 The accuracy of the name Winor is questionable - the handwritten source is unclear at this point.

Luttman served in the First World War (Sub-Lt. RNVR from May 1918 to April 1919) was also Principal of St Albans School of Music, founded by his predecessor. He founded St Albans Bach Choir in 1924, which flourishes to this day and has since been directed by all of his successors at the cathedral.

Cuthbert Edward Osmond, 1930–7
(b. Alderbury, Wiltshire, 1904; d. St Albans, 12 January 1937) appears to have been a prodigy, for at the age of 12, he was organist of Nunton, near Salisbury and served as an articled pupil to Dr W. G. Alcock at Salisbury Cathedral, becoming his assistant from 1917 to 1927. During this time he took a degree (Durham BMus,1925) and in 1926 gained both the ARCO and FRCO diplomas, being awarded the highest marks in organ playing ever given by the College up to that time. During Osmond's illness in 1936, and until his successor arrived in 1937, K. F. Malcolmson was temporary organist.

[Kenneth Forbes Malcolmson, 1936–7
(b. London, 29 April, 1911 – d.19 August, 1995) was educated at Eton College, The Royal College of Music and was organ scholar of Exeter College, Oxford, graduating with a BA (1934), BMus (1933) and MA (1938) and the FRCO diploma (1936). After helping out at St Albans during Osmond's final illness he moved to Halifax Parish Church in 1937 and on to Newcastle Cathedral as organist (1938–55), finally becoming Precentor and director of music at Eton College in 1956 until his retirement in 1971.]

Albert Charles Tysoe, 1937–47
(b. 1884, d. Chichester, 22 May 1962, aged 78).

Before his appointment to St Albans, Tysoe had been organist of Leeds Parish Church from 1920 and before that All Saints', Northampton. He took the Durham degrees of BMus (1909) and DMus (1915), and held the FRCO diploma. He conducted the Halifax Choral Society from 1922 to 1937.

(Albert) Meredith Davies, CBE, 1947–9
(b. Birkenhead, Cheshire, 30 July 1922, d. New Alresford, Hampshire, 9 March 2005).

Davies entered the junior department of the Royal College of Music as an exhibitioner at the age of eight as a cellist. But he soon showed an interest in the organ, and was taken as a pupil by the great organist George Thalben-Ball. In 1936 he was admitted as a Fellow to the Royal College of Organists (and was awarded the silver medal of the Worshipful Company of Musicians), eventually going up to Oxford as an organ scholar (Keble College, 1941) where he read philosophy, politics, and economics. He was called up for National Service in 1942 and served for three years in the Royal Artillery, returning to Keble after the war where he took the degrees of BA (1946), BMus (1946), and MA (1947).

His first appointment was as organist of St Albans Cathedral, 1947–9, but he soon moved on at Hereford Cathedral in 1950, succeeding Sir Percy Hull. He was encouraged by Sir Adrian Boult to become a full-time conductor and the Dean and Chapter at Hereford were enlightened enough to send him to study advanced conducting in Rome in 1954.

In 1956 he moved to Oxford as organist and supernumerary fellow of New College. While holding this post he became associate conductor of the City of Birmingham Symphony Orchestra, 1957–9, and conductor of the City of Birmingham Choir in 1957, a post which he retained until 1964. He left New College in 1959 to devote himself to conducting.

Perhaps his most important achievement was as conductor of the first performance of Benjamin Britten's *War Requiem* at the opening ceremonies of the new Coventry Cathedral in 1962. He was for some time prominently associated as a conductor with Britten's music, especially the operas when he was music director of the English Opera Group (1962–4). He also conducted at Covent Garden and Sadler's Wells, and from 1964 to 1971 he was conductor of the Vancouver Symphony Orchestra, while continuing free-lance work in the United Kingdom and abroad. He was chief conductor of the BBC Training Orchestra, 1969–72. In 1972 he became conductor of the Royal Choral Society. He took up the post of principal of Trinity College of Music in 1979, was appointed CBE in 1982, and retired in 1988.

(Claud) Peter Primrose Burton, 1950–7
(b. Shere, Surrey 1916, d. Hemel Hempstead, Hertfordshre, 6 July 1957).

After war-service, Burton took up his first important post as organist of St Mary's, Warwick and music master of Warwick School in 1946, remaining there until 1950. He had been student at the Royal College of Music and a pupil of W. H. Harris before going up to St John's College, Oxford in 1933, and he took the degrees of BA, BMus (1938) and MA (1943). He held the FRCO and CHM diploma. His untimely death in office from tuberculosis at the age of 41 was precipitated by attempting to help a chorister who had got into difficulty while swimming.

Masters of the Music of St Albans Cathedral (1958–present)

In the 1960s the title was changed to Master of the Music in order to reflect the breadth of the role and in particular the importance of the work with the Cathedral Choir.

Peter John Hurford, OBE, 1958–78
(b. Minehead, Somerset, 22 November 1930).

Born on St Cecilia's Day, he left Blundell's School in 1948 for the Royal College of Music, where he studied for a year before going as organ scholar to Jesus College, Cambridge (1949–53). He read for part I of the music tripos and part II of the law tripos, and took the FRCO diploma in 1949, and the Cambridge degrees of BA (1953), MA (1956), and MusB (1958). His first appointment was as organist of Holy Trinity Church, Leamington Spa (1956). He left Leamington at the end of 1957, and took up duties at St Albans Cathedral in 1958. Here he made a distinctive contribution, first by being the driving force behind the acquisition of the Harrison & Harrison organ (1962, which he co-designed with Ralph Downes) and by his foundation of the International Organ Festival in 1963, which continues to flourish and of which he is still President.

In 1967–8 he was organist-in-residence at the University of Cincinnati, and was visiting professor at the University of Western Ontario, 1976–7. Since leaving St Albans Cathedral he has continued his activities as a recitalist in the UK, Europe, Japan, Australia, New Zealand, Canada, and the USA. In 1981 he was made an honorary doctor of Baldwin-Wallace College, Ohio (home of the Riemenschneider Bach Institute). He has since been awarded a number of honorary doctorates.

Hurford has a formidable reputation as a solo organist and is, to this day, best known for his interpretations of the organ music of J.S. Bach, having recorded the complete organ works for both Decca and BBC Radio 3. His performances are notable for his attention to stylistic detail, clear articulation, expression, and lively tempi. He has also published a good deal of organ music and choral music for the Anglican church. His setting of Robert Herrick's poem *A Litany to the Holy Spirit* for treble voices is an exquisite miniature and is still sung world-wide.

He was President of the Royal College of Organists (1980–82), appointed OBE in 1984, and is the author of *Making Music on the Organ* (1988). He was made an honorary Fellow of Jesus College Cambridge in 2006.

[Simon John Preston, 1967–8

(b. Bournemouth, Hants, 4 August 1938)
Preston was acting Master of the Music at St Albans Cathedral during Peter Hurford's sabbatical year in the USA (September 1967–July 1968). He was educated at Canford School, the Royal Academy of Music and King's College Cambridge (organ student) taking his BA (1961), MusB (1962) and MA (1964). From 1962 to 1967 he was sub-organist of Westminster Abbey, and then in 1970 he became organist and Student of Christ Church, Oxford and a tutor and lecturer in music. He returned to Westminster Abbey as organist in 1981, leaving in 1987 to follow a career as an internationally renowned concert organist.]

Stephen Mark Darlington, 1978–85 (b. Lapworth, Warwickshire 21 September 1952)

Darlington was educated at the King's School, Worcester and Christ Church, Oxford as organ scholar (1971–74) gaining an FRCO (1972) taking a BA in music (1974) and MA (1976). From 1974–8 he was assistant organist of Canterbury Cathedral, and then became Master of the Music at St Albans and the second Artistic Director of the IOF until his return to Oxford in 1985 as organist and Student of Christ Church and a tutor and lecturer in music, where he has remained since. He was President of the Royal College of Organists (1998–2000) and he is currently Choragus of the University of Oxford. He is the holder of a Lambeth Doctorate in Music.

Colin Stephen Walsh, 1985–8
(b. Portsmouth, Hampshire, 26 January 1955).

Walsh was educated at Portsmouth Grammar School, then was organ scholar at St George's Chapel, Windsor Castle before going up to Christ Church, Oxford as organ scholar (1974–8) gaining an FRCO (1976), and taking the degree of BA and later MA. He was assistant organist at Salisbury Cathedral from 1978 until he moved to St Albans in 1985, where he was also the third artistic director of the IOF. He moved to Lincoln Cathedral as Organist three years later where he has remained since, becoming the Organist Laureate in 2003. He also pursues a career as a concert organist.

Barry Michael Rose, OBE, 1988–1997
(b. Chingford, Essex, 24 May 1934)

Though strongly attracted to music (especially the music of the Church of England) from an early age, Rose did not at first become a full-time professional musician. However, from boyhood he had held several posts in church music: organist of St Anne's, Chingford, 1946–56; choirman in Hampstead Parish Church, 1956–7; organist of St Andrew's, Kingsbury, London, 1957–60. In 1958 he entered the Royal Academy of Music, studying there until 1960, with C. H. Trevor as his organ teacher. It was while he was a student there that he was appointed to Guildford Cathedral as its first organist. In 1971 he was also appointed to be music adviser to the head of religious broadcasting at the BBC, a post he held until the 1990s. In 1974 he became sub-organist of St Paul's Cathedral and from 1977–84 was master of the choir, directing the cathedral choir at the wedding of the Prince and Princess of Wales in 1981. He left St Paul's in 1984 and was master of the choirs at King's School, Canterbury until 1988.

He took up his appointment as Master of the Music at St Albans in September 1988 and it was during Rose's time at St Albans that the Abbey Girls Choir was founded (1996). He retired on Christmas Day 1997 to Somerset but has maintained an active career as a specialist choral director in Anglican Church music throughout the world and especially in the USA. He was awarded an honorary doctorate by the City University (London) and is also a Fellow of the Royal Academy of Music (FRAM) and a Fellow of the Royal School of Church Music (FRSCM). In 1998 he was awarded an OBE for services to cathedral music.

Andrew Lucas, 1998–present
(b. Wellington, Shropshire, 19 August 1958)

Lucas was educated at the Wakeman School, Shrewsbury and the Royal College of Music gaining an FRCO (1979) and the degree of BMus (London) (1981). He was assistant organist at three London churches (St Mary Abbots, Kensington, St James, Paddington and St Michael, Cornhill) and later director of music at two: St James, Paddington (1981) and St Vedast-alias-Foster in the City of London (1986) as well as organ student (1980), assistant sub-organist (1985) and then sub-organist and assistant director of music (1990–98) of St Paul's Cathedral, London. In the latter role he made over twenty-five CD recordings, accompanying the cathedral choir in their acclaimed series of English Cathedral music.

He moved to St Albans in February 1998, was sixth artistic director of the IOF (1999–2007) and is the current music director of St Albans Bach Choir (since January 1998). In 1999 he founded the Abbey Singers (a youth choir, mainly of recent ex-choristers of both choirs) and, as the artistic adviser, was instrumental in the latest restoration and enlargement of the Cathedral's Harrison & Harrison organ.

Sunday Afternoon Organ Concerts 2016
at 3pm in St Albans Cathedral

Admission free

20 March at 3pm
James McVinnie
(Concert Organist)

17 July at 3pm
Andrew Lucas
(Master of the Music, St Albans Cathedral)

14 August at 3pm
Tom Winpenny
(Assistant Master of the Music, St Albans Cathedral)

23 October at 3pm
Roger Sayer
(Organist and Director of Music, The Temple Church, London)

Admission to the concerts is free.
A retiring collection helps to support music in the Cathedral.

---

4 December at 5.15pm
Tom Winpenny plays Messiaen's *La Nativité du Seigneur*

Also of interest:
Bank Holiday Monday, 2nd May at 1pm
BRASS & ORGAN SPECTACULAR
with **Prime Brass** and **Tom Winpenny** (organ)

THE CATHEDRAL ORGAN was built in 1962 to a design by Peter Hurford (then Master of the Music) and Ralph Downes. The design of the instrument was revolutionary, being the first cathedral instrument in Britain to be voiced and built on neo-classical lines, whilst being flexible for accompanying the traditional English cathedral repertoire. In 2007-2009 the organ was comprehensively refurbished by Harrison & Harrison of Durham (the original builders), and the specification may be found overleaf.

The organ is the centrepiece of the biennial **St Albans International Organ Festival and Competitions**, founded by Peter Hurford in 1963. For details of the **Festival** and its series of **Saturday Celebrity Organ Concerts**, please go to: www.organfestival.com

The Harrison & Harrison Organ in St Albans Cathedral

PEDAL ORGAN

1.	Sub Bass	32
2. ‡	Principal	16
3.	Major Bass	16
4.	Bourdon	16
5.	Quint	102/3
6. ‡	Octave	8
7.	Gedeckt	8
8.	Nazard	51/3
9.	Choral Bass	4
10.	Open Flute	2
11.	Mixture 19.22.26.29	IV
12. *	Fagotto	32
13.	Bombardon	16
14.	Bass Trumpet (from 41)	16
15. *	Fagotto (from 12)	16
16.	Tromba	8
17.	Shawm	4

i Choir to Pedal   ii Great to Pedal
iii Swell to Pedal   iv Solo to Pedal

CHOIR ORGAN

18.	Quintaton	16
19.	Open Diapason	8
20.	Gedacktpommer	8
21.	Flauto Traverso	8
22.	Octave	4
23.	Rohr Flute	4
24.	Wald Flute	2
25.	Larigot	11/3
26.	Sesquialtera 19.24/12.17	II
27. †	Mixture 22.26.29.33	IV
28.	Cromorne	8

v Tremulant   vi Octave   vii Unison off
viii Swell to Choir   ix Solo to Choir

* new additions, 2009
† restored or revised ranks, 2009
‡ new façade pipes, 2009
Manual compass 58 notes; pedal compass 32 notes

GREAT ORGAN

29. ‡	Principal	16
30.	Bourdon	16
31. ‡	Principal	8
32. ‡	Diapason	8
33.	Spitzflute	8
34.	Stopped Diapason	8
35.	Octave	4
36.	Stopped Flute	4
37.	Quint	22/3
38.	Super Octave	2
39.	Blockflute	2
40. †	Mixture 19.22.26.29	IV-VI
41.	Bass Trumpet	16
42. *	Trumpet	8
43. *	Clarion	4
44.	Grand Cornet 1.8.12.15.17. (tenor g)	V

x Choir to Great
xi Swell to Great   xii Solo to Great

SWELL ORGAN

45.	Open Diapason	8
46.	Rohr Flute	8
47.	Viola	8
48.	Celeste (tenor c)	8
49.	Principal	4
50.	Open Flute	4
51.	Nazard	22/3
52. *	Octave	2
53.	Gemshorn	2
54.	Tierce	13/5
55. †	Mixture 22.26.29	III
56. *	Cimbel 29.33.36	III
57.	Corno di Bassetto	16
58.	Hautboy	8
59.	Vox Humana	8
60.	Trumpet	8
61.	Clarion	4

xiii Tremulant xiv Octave
xv Sub Octave xvi Unison Off

SOLO ORGAN

62.	Fanfare Trumpet	8
63.	Grand Cornet (from Great)	V
64.	Corno di Bassetto (from Swell)	16

xvii Octave xviii Unison off
xix Great Reeds on Solo
* Cimbelstern

NAVE ORGAN (prepared)

65. *	Bourdon (bass from 72)	16
66. *	Principal	8
67. *	Rohr Flute	8
68. *	Octave	4
69. *	Spitzflute	4
70. *	Super Octave	2
71. *	Mixture 19.22.26.29	IV
72. *	Pedal Sub Bass	16

xx Nave on Great   xxi Nave on Solo

THE CATHEDRAL AND ABBEY CHURCH OF SAINT ALBAN

Cathedral and Abbey Church of St Alban
Sumpter Yard, St Albans, Hertfordshire, AL1 1BY
Tel +44 (0)1727 860780
E-mail: mail@stalbanscathedral.org

January 2016
Leaflet design: Colin Innes-Hopkins 01727 854731